Back in the Game

My Year of Dating Dangerously

KELLY GREEN

BACK IN THE GAME
My Year of Dating Dangerously

ISBN 978-1-61961-395-9 *Paperback*
      978-1-61961-396-6 *Ebook*

LIONCREST
PUBLISHING

DEDICATED TO MY TRIBE AND MY GUIDE

Contents

I wrote this book from the notes of my personal journal and the best recollection of my memory. I consulted with most, but not, all characters in the book to review details and chronological events so that it is written as true and accurate as possible. I have changed the names of most, but not all, of the individuals, and, in some cases, I also modified identifying details in order to preserve anonymity. There are no composite characters. In one instance, one character is placed in an event in oder to best hide their identity. I occasionally omitted people and events, but only when that omission had no impact on the interest of the story.

Back in the Game

Introduction

MY COMING OUT PARTY

"It's fun to have fun but you have to know how."

DR. SEUSS

It is pitch black. The faint buzz of traffic is punctuated by honking horns. My mouth is dry. Where the hell am I? My head is pounding and my ears throbbing, side effects of too much champagne. Am I alone? Damn eye mask. I struggle to remove it, caught in my tangled hair. Searching for an ounce of familiarity, I spot my favorite studded heels near the bed. I wore them last night with the new Balmain dress given to me just for this special evening. I flop my hand over the side of the bed, searching for my phone while attempting to minimize the throbbing inside my skull.

A faint feeling of dread and anxiety subsume me. I am disappointed in myself, and I don't want to get out of bed and face the day.

7:03 am. I calculate I've had about three hours of sleep. The space next to me has clearly been slept in, but it's empty now. I roll over on my side, sandwiching my head with a pillow as I recount the events of the previous evening. They brought me to understand the road ahead of me will be long and tumultuous, and I don't want to think about it any longer.

Austin, Texas, a beautiful fall day—11/11, 2013. My friend Kim invited me to attend a birthday party in New York City. It was a spur of the moment trip we decided to take only the day before. Neither of us had time to pack properly, but I was ready to embrace spontaneity and adventure.

The invitation came at a time when I was still processing the end of a ten-year marriage. I was broken and beaten down, and my life was in total disarray. The realities of my responsibilities had left me like a ghost of my usual self. I grasped for any sort of goodness in my life, and my friends were there to support me. Kim thought that this one-night trip might be a good chance for me to break that cycle by having some fun at a memorable party in the city that never sleeps.

✳ ✳ ✳

It is mid-morning on this crisp fall day, and I'm the first to arrive at the airport's private Atlantic Aviation, where the pilot of the Challenger aircraft greets me and leads me onboard. I don't fly private often, but I do know it is proper etiquette on a private plane not to select the best seat, so I'm nervously milling around, waiting for Kim to show up and select hers first. In the meantime, Nak Armstrong arrives with a bottle of champagne. Nak is the ultimate gentleman and has been a good friend. Most women clamor for a friendship with Nak, an award-winning jewelry designer who sells his work to upscale boutiques like Barneys New York. He tells me he's meeting with *Vogue* in the city, but he's also coming to the party tonight, and I'm thrilled to be in his company.

We are running a tad late when Kim bursts onto the plane in sunglasses, carrying a Birkin bag and her signature venti Starbucks green tea. She is a graceful Southern woman, full of grit. Her glass blue eyes give warmth to her petite athletic build. She is on a call, but she cups her hand to cover the phone and greet us.

"Good morning, sweetie! I hope you are ready for an exciting evening," she says to me.

Kim's neighborhood Starbucks has affectionately named her Phone Lady. She is a ball of eternal energy and an inspiration to many women. She's not only a mother of two daughters, but also a fantastic artist and a force in the music industry. After sharing hugs and kisses, we talk about how we're all amped up about the party, but the night has an added edge for me. It's my first significant social event since becoming single again. This is my reintroduction to the world of dating, and to be honest, I'm scared shitless. I do my best to cover this up in front of my friends, because tonight isn't about me. It is about the party.

The decadence of being on a private plane combined with my nerves fuel my desire to celebrate my coming-out-of-sorts with a glass of wine or a cocktail. Kim, however, has other ideas: she insists that there's no drinking on the plane because it's going to be a long night. I'm in no mood to argue, especially as a guest on this adventure. When Kim calls the shots, we all listen. As the plane takes off, I reach for a bag of cashews. Nak shakes his head and wags his index finger, stopping me in my tracks.

"Oh, honey, you cannot eat salted nuts on an airplane," he says. "You're going to be in a tight dress tonight, which means you'll blow up like a blowfish, so no salty nuts for you."

Have they been conspiring ahead of time to help me make it through the evening? I sip my boring water and realize that such a plan probably has a purpose.

Eventually, I decide to relax. While my mind drifts, sleep finds me. I wake three hours later as we land in Teterboro, New Jersey. Like me, the others have just woken from a nap, so the ride into New York largely passes in silence. It's early evening as we coast down the West Side Highway of Manhattan. To our right is a beautiful sunset overlooking the Hudson River, which we observe in silent wonderment. Our first stop for the evening is the Maritime Hotel, where we plan to prep for the evening. In typical Kim style, nothing is half-assed: she has arranged a trio of professional stylists to get us ready for the party.

Barneys has sent a stylist named Faustin, a Frenchman who speaks English through an accent so thick I can barely understand what he's saying. Alongside him is the hairstylist—another Frenchman—and lastly, a well-known Armani makeup artist named Rafael. Faustin has brought a rack of what can be best described as the slinkiest of slinky disco dresses for us to choose from. The team is busy milling about, looking at Kim and me, sizing up the task. I mope, feeling like they've got their work cut out for them, trying to turn a mutt into a thoroughbred.

Faustin takes control of the room and commands us to try on the dresses, and of course, Nak is there to help give his approval, checking everything with his perfectionist eye. It's been years since I've felt this pampered, and I'm loving it. Kim and I giggle at the boisterous conversation in the room. After she makes her dress selection, the room unanimously decides I should wear an *extremely* short, body-hugging dress. It's probably the shortest dress I've ever worn in my life. I'm ecstatic with how I look and the self-confidence Kim has rapidly bestowed on me. I'm thrilled to be having this experience with my friends—but at the same time, my internal monologue is running wild. I'm overwhelmed, scared and nervous about what's to come.

In a way, I can't believe that this is where my life is now. I'm so used to being in a monogamous relationship that the thought of trying to snap out of that ingrained mindset is no easy task. Preparing to return to the single world is surreal. Kim pops a bottle of champagne. I am eager to celebrate, but I can't shake the thought that a large part of me is still mourning my marriage. Although that dissolution was one of the most traumatic things I've experienced, I've never been one to linger in negativity. I have a curiosity that I allow to take over and explore what life will bring me. With that in mind, I'm also very much looking forward to this next chapter of my life.

Once Rafael completes our makeup, the coterie of French stylists steps back and as one, they give us a very approving look. They're clearly proud of their work, as they smile and speak French at a rapid pace. We have no idea what they're saying, but they're giddy for us, and perhaps living vicariously through us at the thought of attending what I've come to think of as my coming-out party. In actuality, the spotlight will be on the birthday boy, Leonardo DiCaprio, as tonight's celebration is in honor of his 39th birthday.

Leo's party at Tao kicks off at 10.00 pm. As a mother of four young children, that's usually my bedtime, but since the kids are in Austin with their father, I'm geared up for a night that's well outside my regular, suburban routine. Thankfully, the Maritime Hotel is right around the corner from the venue, because it's mid-November and New York City is freezing. The cold northeasterly air whips against my bare legs. I look and feel absolutely ridiculous in this short skirt, but I've made my bed, so I'll lie in it. No turning back now!

Standing on 9th Street outside Tao, I side-eye some much younger girls lingering on the corner. I can't help but have a nasty thought that they look like imported hookers. I share this with Kim, and we laugh—until she points out that I don't look too dissimilar from those girls. This comment shuts me up quickly and reminds me that my expectations for this night are low—that way, it's harder to be disappointed. Despite my come-hither attire, sex or romance is the last thing on my mind. Instead, I'm looking forward to enjoying a fun evening at a trendy new club.

Inside the venue, the owner, who is hosting this epic party for Leo, warmly greets us. Tao is a huge restaurant, particularly by New York City standards: it's a multi-tiered wonder of a room. Tonight the dinner tables have been removed and it has a special configuration, featuring a central stage and dance floor surrounded by a U-shape of tufted black leather booths and tables that create a sumptuous lounge area. There are around 300 people filling the space, so it has the feel of a highly exclusive event, and I certainly feel privileged to be here.

As we descend into the room, the first people we encounter appear to be female models. Lots of them. They are all very young, very thin, and very gorgeous. They're stacked wall-to-wall, looking around at each other and giving off the unmistakable and familiar vibe of uncertainty and nervousness. They also look bitter and angry. I wonder: how can a person be so vapid at Leonardo DiCaprio's birthday party? This makes me laugh, so I cup my hand to Kim's ear and whisper, "They look so angry. Perhaps they haven't eaten in days". She smiles and spanks me on the ass to keep me moving toward our table. I know a part of me feels absent as well. I wonder if it shows face as it does on theirs.

As we continue down the staircase, we encounter another layer of partygoers, some of whom I recognize as Victoria's Secret models. Here, there's more of a balance between wealthy businessmen and women, and both sexes are mingling amid the plush enclaves of private tables separated by velvet drapes. At the bottom of the staircase is the final layer of the party, which features the dance floor and U-shaped booths with open backs and lounge area. We are shown to our table, which is the first booth and closest to Leo's center table. As we settle in, I look at Leo, who seems quite pleased with the evening so far. As expected, he's in the middle of the party with his favorite friends, surrounded by tiers of partygoers. He is smiling aimlessly in his infamous pageboy hat. Tonight certainly has the feel of a modern-day *Great Gatsby*-style affair.

I'm not generally a star-struck person, but at this point, the celebrity watching is unbelievable. I'm sitting there, taking it all in: the booths surrounding us contain various VIPs such as a Middle Eastern prince and a well-known, uber-wealthy tech mogul. The evening's entertainment is seated in the booth on our left. Kanye West is performing later that night, and he sits calmly with his soon-to-be wife by his side. It appears as though he's trying to get in his zone rather than getting wild. Kim has only recently given birth to their daughter North, so it's quite enchanting to see them out in public.

What strikes me about Tao is the hologram of a Hindu goddess whose arms and eyes are constantly moving. It feels like she's watching me, and me alone, despite the hundreds of people who are noisily filling the room. It's bizarre, yet comforting, to have this omniscient, heavenly creature looking over me as I begin the long, hard process of digging myself out of a social and emotional hole. In a room full of people I somehow feel alone. Looking up at her, I make a silent vow to try to embrace whatever this night will bring—good or bad.

I'm also struck by what a mastermind Leonardo DiCaprio is, as a philanthropist and a fundraiser. Everyone at this party serves a purpose, and he has obviously used all of his God-given natural resources to create this situation, where ideally everyone will have a good time. The party is ultimately a charity event and will benefit the Leonardo DiCaprio Foundation, which focuses on the most pressing environmental issues of our day and restoring balance to threatened ecosystems.

By my estimation, most of the models are here for décor and eye candy, while the celebrities and athletes are here to increase notoriety. The overall effect is to create the buzz of an exclusive guest list, desired by many. Finally, he has hand-picked the wealthy donors who have one thing in common, other than money: they *love* to party. Alongside the prince, it is our role to donate by bidding in an auction. Only Leo could get away with having the wealthiest people in the room bid exclusively on something as simple as champagne. There are no fantasy trips or prizes, just the opportunity to flex your wallet in a room full of beautiful women and celebrities. In the process, his birthday celebration raises millions of dollars. He is simply a genius.

One of Leo's interests with his foundation is to preserve international wildlife on the brink of extinction. I smile to myself when this is announced, as I find it a little ironic that here at Tao, Leo has created a wildlife sanctuary for himself, if only for one night. The predators are the high rollers looking to boost their egos with large donations that might help to attract the prey: the meek, bitter, young models I smirked at on the way in. I had to wonder, though: in this wildlife sanctuary, was I predator or prey? I glance up at the Hindu goddess projected onto the ceiling. She stares back at me, offering no answer.

While I ponder this question, the party continues to warm up. I'm sipping my preferred drink—Patrón and soda—and I've found a secure perch atop the back of our booth. I try to blend in as I awkwardly drape my naked legs over the seat. To my back is an open space, and brushing my shoulders are Orlando Bloom and Kristen Wiig. I feel like an unpopular teenager as I timidly watch over them. The scene mesmerizes me as Kristen exchanges some sort of homemade gift with Orlando, who has only recently announced his separation from his wife, Miranda Kerr. Watching Orlando, my heart softens as I feel a great amount of empathy for him in this moment, and I wonder to myself whether, as a newly single man, he's feeling like I do—a curious mixture of nervousness, fear and shyness, perhaps?

I barely have time to finish formulating this thought before a group of four gorgeous young blondes rally around him and bust out a choreographed dance routine, topped off with some highly sexual booty drops. I laugh at the scene and realize that no, Orlando Bloom is not having the same issues as I am; in fact, he's going to be just fine.

Orlando's presence and sexual confidence bring light to the fact that I haven't flirted with another man since my divorce. I haven't even entertained the thought of looking for another man. I certainly haven't been touched by another person in months. Sitting there, in the center of an extraordinary social situation, I feel naïve and unprepared for what lies ahead. What do people talk about when they're at the club? What do people talk about when they're on *dates*? These situations are completely foreign to me as a 42-year-old, newly single woman—though one who forever feels like a 27-year-old at heart.

As the room fills, the volume of the music is gradually bumped up, which entices the crowd to inch closer to the dance floor. Kim and Kanye's booth is completely packed—naturally—but ours still has a little spare room, which a few interlopers keep trying to take advantage of. Our space has been assigned its own security guard, a huge and friendly guy who is happy enough to remove people if we say the word. Feeling a bit paralyzed, I haven't moved from my high seat when I feel a creeper slink over to my left side. He is sitting so close to me that our legs are touching. I tense up at the physical contact, but he says nothing, so I begin to wonder if his "move" is intentional or unintentional. I try to relax and enjoy the warmth of his leg against mine, but I am decidedly creeped-out. My defenses are raised.

I strain my neck up making eye contact with the security guard. I'm about to ask him to kick this guy out when, thankfully, Nak sees what's happening and quickly intervenes by stroking my hair and saying, "Sweetie, you need to relax. Just enjoy the party and enjoy the moment. You don't need to kick people out—particularly if it's Ed Norton." Sure enough, he's right: Ed is sitting with his girlfriend, deep in conversation and completely unaware of my presence. I realize I am a simpleton. Edward was clearly not making a move on me. I breathe a sigh of relief. A sigh of stupidity and realize that Nak is correct, as usual: I *do* need to relax, as I'm wound up way too tightly for a party that I told myself I'd try to enjoy, no matter what.

Kim proudly prances back to the table, bringing with her a winning catch: a couple of handsome guests. She introduces me to a tall, broad-shouldered guy who is ridiculously fit. His eyes are an indescribable color, a cross between hazel and gray; they seem to change color at a moment's notice. He's wearing jeans and an untucked button-down shirt. We shake hands and I can't help but notice how powerful yet warm his hand feel. He introduces himself as Alex. Since I don't live in Manhattan and I don't follow sports, it doesn't click that I've just met Alex Rodriguez—A-Rod—infamous for his trail of beauties and generally scandalous behavior. We stand in the booth and become acquainted before he asks if I want to sit down. At his suggestion, I take my safe spot back, so now I'm tightly squeezed between Ed Norton and A-Rod. It's certainly a bit of a departure from my regular

Sunday night on the couch watching HBO.

Immediately, I'm struck by his disarming charm; he doesn't come across in a gross, Rico Suave sort of way. He's so grounded and well-mannered that he makes me feel like I'm the only person in the room. He appears to be genuinely interested in what I have to say, as he's the one leading the conversation. His opening line is a little cheesy: "I wanted to come over to the table because you and your friend Kim are the most beautiful women at this party." I raise an eyebrow in response, as I think to myself: *Sure*, we both saw the tiers of gorgeous models that you had to walk through to get to this spot.

His next line only causes me to raise my eyebrow further: "I am so tired of these wafer-thin New York girls that look as though they haven't eaten. You girls look healthy." Hang on—is *healthy* a compliment, or is he calling me fat? How healthy? I lighten up and laugh, thinking to myself that perhaps we have something in common: I had actually made the same observation earlier.

He quickly glosses over these opening remarks by asking me to talk about myself. My immediate reaction is to run away from that question. 'Me' is a mess right now; I'd rather talk about literally anything else. What could I say? "I'm 42 years old, divorced, and so uptight that I nearly kicked Ed Norton out of my booth after he accidentally brushed his leg against mine?" Yikes!

Rather than answer his question directly, I deflect by offering him a drink—which he quickly declines, as he's in training. Of course; I'm an idiot, he's a professional athlete, why would he be drinking alcohol? Can I possibly make this more awkward? He asks whether I drink a lot. I pause to ponder the question. Does he mean tonight, or in general? Not *a lot*, I reply, but I do drink. He asks whether I smoke, and I truthfully say no, to which he replies with a smile, "Yeah, I didn't think so." This exchange is a little strange; it's almost like he is trying to qualify me against a set of criteria he has sketched out in his mind for the types of women that he wants to have in his life. I wait for the next question to leave his lips.

He mentions again that I look "healthy," and he asks what I like to eat, which begins our bonding over my enjoyment of cooking. As an athlete, he's clearly focused on healthy eating, and he seems genuinely excited when I begin talking about my fondness for cooking crockpot Paleo dishes like jerk pork, Thai beef, and Mexican chicken. When he tells me that he also enjoys cooking, we're plunged deep into a conversation that involves comparing recipes. I have become oblivious to my surroundings. When I look up, I notice a small man standing close behind us. Alex tells me not to worry; that's his bodyguard. He just so happens to be about a quarter of Alex's size, and I wonder what he could possibly protect him from. Alex reads my mind and bobs his head to motion behind him. I lean over slightly and notice a line of no less than seven girls waiting to speak to him. My eyes widen. The small guard smiles at me, as if to say, "I've got your back."

This conversation is a real 'pinch me' sort of moment: I imagine there aren't any other people here at Leo's 39th birthday party talking about their favorite crockpot dishes, yet Alex is so engaging and easy to talk to that it feels completely natural. I can't help but think that he's just a nice guy who's looking for a quality girl to marry. How sweet!

By this point, I have totally lost all sense of what else is going on around us, because I'm so absorbed by the conversation and those beautiful eyes. Our small talk turns to what I like to do in my spare time, and when I begin my answer with the words, "When I'm not with the kids…," I don't even get to finish my sentence before he stops me and says, "Wait, you have kids?"

The smartest part of my dumb, newly single mind realizes that this is not the kind of conversation that I should be having right now, so I try to backpedal a little, but he grins and says, "That's great! What are their ages?" All of a sudden, I'm feeling nervous and sweaty, like a big, hot spotlight has been flicked on directly above me, ready to broadcast my answer to the whole party. "Five, five, three and two," I say quietly, half expecting Alex to stop talking to me and begin chatting up one of the wafer-thin, childless New York girls he had previously talked smack about.

But again, A-Rod surprises me. He's super-positive in response, so much so that he pulls out his phone and begins showing me pictures of his two young girls, as any proud father would. It's clear that they're the light of his life, just as my children are mine. He asks to see pictures of my kids, so I pull out my phone, and in the process I dimly register that the time is now 3:40 am. We've been engrossed in this conversation for so long that I've completely lost all sense of time. As I begin flipping through pictures of my kids, Nak and Kim are both shooting death stares in my direction. I can hear them both silently yelling in my ear: "Are you *seriously* whipping out photos of your children in the middle of this party right now?!"

Okay, they have a point: this probably isn't the greatest way to attract one of the country's top athletes. But as far as I'm concerned, I'm doing nothing more than having a pleasant conversation with an engaging guy—who just happens to be gorgeous and one of Manhattan's most eligible bachelors. He *is* eligible, right? I haven't quite gotten up to date on that question.

As I put my phone away and begin refocusing on the room—where Kanye West is on stage with 2 Chainz; a once-in-a-lifetime event that I should be paying attention to—A-Rod slides his hand around my waist, pulling me closer to him. By now, I'm less skittish than I was after my earlier brush with Ed Norton, but my ability to read flirting must be off. I can't tell whether it's an affectionate grab or whether he's using this physical contact to try to mentally calculate my body fat percentage.

I finally have the good sense to know that it's time for me to break this moment by standing up and doing a little shimmy, eager to shake off that awkward and reasonably inappropriate conversation about my domestic life. I move away from him and start dancing, which confuses Alex, as he's not sure whether to take this as a sign that I've given up on our conversation. Kanye's song 'Stronger' is booming through the speakers. He prowls the stage confidently, microphone in hand, as the crowd mirrors his famous chorus back to him:

> *N-now th-that that don't kill me*
> *Can only make me stronger*
> *I need you to hurry up now*
> *'Cause I can't wait much longer*

Eventually, Alex joins me on the dance floor after watching

me for a little while. He grabs me and pulls me close to him, but I'm not responding appropriately. To be honest, I'm confused by the signals he's sending. I'm so out of touch with how sexual attraction between strangers works that I can't read his cues, which must be frustrating for an alpha male who has been a confident sexual being for his entire adult life. In this situation, I certainly feel like prey before a practiced predator.

Eventually he grabs my elbow, puts his hand on the small of my back, just above my butt, and whispers in my ear, "I'll be right back." I watch him gracefully leap over the back of the booth, vaulting across my safe little party perch. I know instantly that I'll never see him again.

It's an awkward way to end our interactions together, as I've been nothing less than enchanted by his charisma and magnetism from the very first moment. He made me feel like I was the light of his universe, for tonight anyway. It was an extremely flattering experience considering how many beautiful women are crowding Tao tonight.

Despite all of my muddled thoughts and emotions, as I watched Alex hop over the booth, I was met by a wave of disappointment and loss. It wasn't so much the fact that I hadn't taken the opportunity to exchange numbers with him; instead, it was more of an internal disappointment for not being able to take control of myself in the moment by responding appropriately. I felt like I possibly fucked up a golden chance to make a connection with a captivating man. A disappointing thought that stayed with me as we walked back to the Maritime Hotel. Meanwhile, the party was still pumping inside, with Leo at the center, surrounded by women, eating up the occasion and reveling in the company of his friends.

* * *

I wake from my five-minute slumber to the sight of Kim bounding into the hotel room with some green juice and a coffee for me. She's already firing on all cylinders, as usual, while I'm barely conscious. Kim, great friend that she is, can tell that I'm still downcast about how last night ended. She strokes my head and says, "You'll do better next time." She lightens the mood by joking that rather than waking up here at the hotel, I could've instead been stuck in traffic on my way back from A-Rod's apartment, with a signed baseball and a jersey in hand. I laugh and start to feel a little better about how it all went down. Maybe it wasn't such a bad night, after all.

Back in Austin a couple of days later, though, Alex is still on my mind, and I can't stop myself from Googling him. I learn that he does have a girlfriend, which gives me mixed feelings about the questionable signals I was receiving a few nights earlier. As I scroll through news stories on my phone, my eye settles on one published on November 13, two days after the party, which details the allegation that he was caught having sex in a bathroom with a girl in Miami.

I'm taken aback. The Alex that I met would never do that. But in a parallel universe—if I had been in a different head-space, and feeling a little more confident about myself and my situation—would that have been me in the bathroom?

Ultimately, I think I dodged a bullet, because I would *not* want to be mentioned in a news story after being caught fucking the world's biggest baseball star in a Miami bathroom. Nonetheless, Leonardo DiCaprio's 39th birthday will be hard to top, and it certainly set the tone for what was to come in 2014—my year of dating dangerously.

One

BABY STEPS

"The most fundamental aggression to ourselves, the most fundamental harm we can do to ourselves, is to remain ignorant by not having the courage and the respect to look at ourselves honestly and gently."

PEMA CHÖDRÖN

Despite what you've just read, I'm just an average urban mom with an out-of-this-world support system who happens to be presented with the occasional tantalizing social opportunity. More often than not, I like to take a chance by saying "yes." I feel that as I navigate this shadowy path to rediscovering myself after a failed marriage, being surrounded by strong friends and an adventurous spirit is more important than ever.

I grew up in Dallas as a fifth-generation Texan. It's certainly true that you can take the girl out of Dallas, but you can't take Dallas out of the girl: I wholeheartedly embrace most of the stereotypes that surround my people, and I've always been fond of dressing myself up to the nines. My father worked in the aviation industry across the USA, Europe, and Africa, while my mother held a series of office jobs throughout my upbringing. My parents divorced early, and I grew up as an only child, although I have two older half-sisters from Dad's first marriage. I was the youngest of my father's daughters. He had the highest hopes for me and affectionately nicknamed me after his father, Charlie, a moniker that still sticks with me today. After their divorce, a single mother raised me in the 1970s. We didn't have a lot of material things, but I had a lot of love in my life. Despite the separation, my parents equally instilled a strong sense of independence and promoted the thought that I could achieve anything in life I sought after. I believed them.

I gave Mom her fair share of headaches. I wasn't a great student, and I was the kind of kid who was constantly sneaking out at night, seeking out illicit fun and looking to enjoy life as much as I could. Mom has assured me in later life, thankfully, that I wasn't a bad kid, but my desire for adolescent exploration was probably more than she was ready to deal with on her own. Despite my lack of academic focus, through my tenacity to explore a bigger life I found myself attending Texas Tech, in the rural western town of Lubbock, where I studied marketing.

By that point in my life, I was more committed to hitting the books and acing tests, partly as a result of growing up with a modest lifestyle and realizing how important an education was if I wanted to achieve the life I dreamed of. When I first arrived at Texas Tech, my lack of academic focus caught up with me. I had to work hard and teach myself how to study, and how to make it in college. After four fun years in college and securing my business degree, I found my way into the booming technology industry of the early 1990s.

In 2015, working in tech is perceived as a sexy profession, but in the '90s barely anyone knew what the hell it was. What I did know is that it paid well, so I pursued that path with a vengeance. I quickly learned what startups and stock options were all about. A couple of company acquisitions later, I was at Cisco Systems while it was still in its incubation stage. There were very few women in the industry at that time: the Cisco Dallas office had 96 people, of which I was one of only two females.

Out of necessity, I learned to survive and compete. Soon enough, I thrived in that environment. Although I experienced my share of sexism in the workplace, I was fortunate enough to have genuine care and guidance from male mentors who were willing to coach a girl they viewed as their sister or daughter.

My career certainly opened up the world for me and exposed me to many new people and cultures. Initially, I thought I'd work in technology sales until I found something else, but here I am, still doing it and still loving it. The technology boom was kind to me and put me in a financial situation that a scrappy girl from a divorced family could only dream of. I had fulfilled my parents' wishes of becoming an independent woman who was more than capable of taking care of myself.

While working in Dallas after college, I became engaged, but I called off the wedding. Looking back, I'm not sure why I ended it. Perhaps it should have been my first clue that my desire for adventure needed to be bridled. Something in my heart told me there was a bigger world out there for me, so I left my home and everything familiar to me and moved to San Francisco, where I stayed for eight years through my late 20s and early 30s. I've had an exhilarating career, traveling extensively through Latin America, Europe, and Asia for business. Work allowed me the opportunity to grow into myself, and become a confident woman. I learned that I could take care of myself in any situation. There are few better feelings than being confident in yourself and in your ability to cope in any situation, no matter what kind of curveball life throws your way.

In San Francisco, I met my husband-to-be, waiting for a table at a sushi restaurant in the Marina district. Mas Sake was known less for good sushi than for its hot waitresses and reputation as a pick-up spot. We were both shy; neither of us wanted to make the first move. Eventually, our friends coaxed us into sitting at a table together. There was an instant connection between us; sparks flew as our knees touched under the table. I dove right into that relationship without hesitation. Our first date was a romantic evening at a Giants baseball game that ended with a drink at the famous Top of the Mark hotel in Nob Hill. After that evening, we were inseparable. We fell in love, and two years later, we had a fairytale wedding overlooking the San Francisco Bay.

A lot of my friends were having children in their late 20s, but at that point, my career was at an all-time high, and I wasn't sure whether I wanted to have kids. For a time, I thought I would be quite content never having children, but as I got into my early 30s, we both decided to start trying to conceive. I soon found out that pregnancy is not something you can control. It took several gut-wrenching years of trying. This was an unwelcome struggle until I eventually became pregnant with twins. We were thrilled with the healthy delivery of our boy-girl combination. Life couldn't be more perfect.

Two years later I became pregnant with our third child—a daughter. She was soon followed by an unexpected—but welcomed—fourth: a boy. Perhaps I am living proof that when you wish for something so much, with so much intensity, it can come to you in abundance. Although I am grateful for my career, becoming a mother of four became my greatest passion in life. These four beautiful little people remained the grounding influence in my life, particularly in the turbulent year after the divorce.

There was a lot going on in marriage: multiple years obsessing over pregnancy topped with three pregnancies back-to-back. In hindsight, I don't think having our hands full with children directly contributed to the downfall of our relationship. There were bigger issues at play, but I think for any couple, those early child-rearing years are an intense and exhausting time, especially when trying to manage two demanding careers in tandem.

So how did I become single again at age 42, as a mother of four small children? That's the question I asked myself over and over in those dreadful first months after the separation. I was sure I had made all the right decisions in life. I became financially stable first, married later than most of my friends, and chose a partner who I thought would be loyal for life. My husband was raised in a wonderful, fun-loving family. He was highly educated, having attended Johns Hopkins and Cal Berkeley. He was five years younger than me, and from the moment we first met, I was impressed by his physicality: he's six-foot-four, with dark, wavy hair and big, blue eyes. He's always been handsome, and that remains true today. Together, I was sure we had the makings of a life lived happily ever after.

After getting married and having children, I lost myself in the struggle of finding true intimacy. I grew up in a generation of women taught to believe independence is the key to a fulfilled life, and it certainly is important. However, I think women today have a challenging time finding a balance between independence and vulnerability. For highly independent women, it's difficult to find and keep intimacy in our personal relationships.

Through the patterns and routines of marriage, I had allowed my identity to be subsumed by an oppressive partnership and perceived notions of marital perfection. I was the quintessential wife. My hobbies included interior decorating, Pilates, the occasional school fundraiser, book club—basically, just a bunch of shit that you think you're supposed to do. I could have been your perfect Pinterest board, in all categories. It was all *fine*, and I enjoyed every bit of it, but it wasn't necessarily living. It was more like existing, striving for this unattainable goal of perfection, what I thought my life was *supposed* to be. We had a fabulous house in Austin, a Range Rover and a BMW parked in the garage, and all the requisite comforts and devices. If you looked at us as a couple, ferrying the kids to their social events, you would have thought that we had it together. Outwardly, we seemed to embody the perfect modern family.

If you could have looked behind closed doors, you would have seen that while we didn't have a bad marriage, it wasn't the perfection we portrayed. I wasn't honest with myself and didn't acknowledge that I needed more. Deep down, I wanted to feel cared for and understood. We were both just surviving and hoping to hold our family together. I was naïve with regard to the severity of my husband's unhappiness. This was abruptly brought to my attention via a text message I happened to catch on his iPad. It was from a young girl in California. I knew the instant I saw the message that my life would never be the same. This was a life-awakening shift that came in a most unexpected way.

My heart sank as I glared at the cold screen. In the reflection, I saw myself becoming frantic. I wondered whether it was a mistake; perhaps the text was intended for someone else? I felt faint and panicked. Having completely lost control of what I had thought was a secure relationship, I paced back and forth with the iPad in hand. I wanted to take some sort of action, but there was nothing to be done. This was a real blip-in-the-matrix sort of moment.

This discovery burst the bubble that had formed around me. I'd falsely believed in the image of our perfect family. My mind searched for answers or for some sort of understanding. My husband and I spent the next year trying to salvage our relationship, but after that rude shock, I had become much more attuned to what was important for me in life, and we both knew that it wasn't going to work. Our differences were irreconcilable; too much had happened, and we were no longer on the same page. I spent that last year of our marriage looking over my shoulder, waiting for the hurtful event. I summoned the courage to wonder how I could reclaim my own identity and happiness.

This was all easier said than done. Divorce is stifling. If you haven't gone through it, it is challenging to truly understand the fear that can consume you. Prior to my own experience, I could not understand the full range of emotions brought on by divorce. My only response to someone getting divorced was simply to say, "I'm so sorry."

Divorce brings questions most people have the luxury of already knowing the answers to, such as: Where will I live? How often will I see my children? Will I be judged as a failure? Which of my friends will stay by my side?

One of the saddest and least acknowledged aspects of divorce is that you don't take the time to mourn the loss or appreciate the good things that you've had together. Fear, possession, and the desire to retain some normalcy takes over. This fear fuels the bitter world of family law. I also now have a deep empathy for those who choose to remain in an unfulfilling relationship. I understand how this fear can stop even the strongest in their tracks and persuade them to tough it out through the most troubled marriage. Only the two people involved can decide what is truly best for them.

I made a conscious decision to grow and learn from the pain and disappointment of the divorce. I knew I had an opportunity to explore my boundaries. I wanted to be open and adventurous and see what the world had in store for me, which paved the way to my year of dating dangerously.

It wasn't as though I went into each of these experiences with the expectation that I'd be learning something, but that's how things unfolded. I allowed myself to be guided by my curiosity. I took every moment I could and asked myself a basic question: does this feel good or not feel good? As I probed my own feelings and actions through the relationships that ensued in 2014, I ended up learning more about my own resilience than I did in all of the previous decade.

* * *

After Leonardo DiCaprio's party and my befuddled encounter with Alex Rodriguez, I realized that I was going to need to return to the dating world in baby steps. Putting myself out there in nightclubs or bars didn't feel right, as that world seemed too trite and hopeless. I thought I'd try the more traditional approach of asking my friends to arrange a date for me. By taking the search out of my hands, I was led to an intriguing guy recommended to me by a close, trusted couple, both of whom spoke highly of him.

I hoped that he would have a good sense of me, as he also grew up in Dallas. Aside from that, I didn't know much else about him other than that he now split his time between Dallas and Europe, where he lives part-time and conducts his business. We both trusted the matchmakers and went for it. On their advice, he rearranged his plans in order to make our date. Before he came in for the weekend, we exchanged a few text messages, where he showed some wit and a sense of fun. I didn't dare let my imagination run away with possibilities, but the excitement was building, and I was looking forward to meeting him.

* * *

On the night of the date, I arrive at my friends' house feeling very Dallas: I'm wearing a pair of black Jimmy Choo booties, grey leggings, and a sweater with a fur collar. Michael is 50, around 5'11," and wears wire glasses, worn jeans, tennis shoes, and a red parka vest that looks as though he bought it in the 90s. He's also wearing a beanie hat, which he soon removes to reveal his bald head. Although my fur and his tattered vest clearly do not match, he manages to appear breezy and confident. Despite my immediate thought of a mismatch, I find that I have an overwhelming sense of attraction to him, a deep connection, as if I've known him for years.

I can barely contain my thoughts. My senses are flooded, and I'm speechless as we come together for the awkward introduction hug and European air kisses. I can hear the familiar-yet-dull voices of my friends. Michael presents them with a gift: a book of some sort. The exchange buys me some time to take things in. His mere presence is immediately comforting, and I have a strong desire to be near him and touch him. My body and senses are saying, "Yes, yes, yes!." My mind is saying, "*Really? What?*" Michael looks nothing like my ex-husband, and nothing like Alex Rodriguez. But I happen to believe in the phenomenon of past lives, and from the very first moment, it's as if there was love in the past.

This is supposed to be an easy date: a throwaway, prac-tice interaction in preparation for meeting someone truly wonderful in the future. I think to myself that I need to get a grip. How could I truly know anything at all about him? We haven't even had a proper conversation. The gift exchange and introductory conversation ends, and I am forced to bring my attention back to the present.

He glances over at me, as if to see that I'm okay, and his deep gaze says more than I've heard from a man in a very long time. We begin the task of getting to know one another by ineptly struggling to connect on a conversational level. He tells me about his recent travel to an orphanage in India; I feel like a shallow fool telling him about my recent travel to a celebrity birthday party in New York. I'm sure he makes a mental note that the cost of my overnight trip could feed a whole village.

He tries a safe zone by discussing current events and mentions that he reads *The New York Times*. Do I dare let him know my primary news sources include DListed, *Perez Hilton*, and *Page Six*? Eventually, we stop trying to make small talk, and he says nothing while stroking the hair around my face. To my surprise, I take comfort in the silence and our awkward connection. I stop worrying about our pairing and relax into the moment.

Our time together is so intoxicating that I barely even interact with my friends. I find myself laughing more than I have in a long time. It isn't that anything is particularly funny, it's just that I feel happy and euphoric. After dinner and a nervous night of too much tequila, he invites me back to his hotel at the Four Seasons. Of course I say yes. Uber drives us there, and after we hop out of the car, we suddenly realize neither of us really knows what we are doing. We hold hands as if we've been a couple for a long time. He confidently leads us into the lobby, then abruptly stops and turns toward me.

We stand face-to-face while our hands explore the new, unfamiliar textures of this potential partnership. The intimacy is intense. I distract myself by noticing the ostentatious Texas decor of the upscale hotel. My eyes dart from the flocked quails to the rope braids that adorn the drapes. I leer at the contrast of the cold, Spanish tiled floor against the warmth of the faux gas fire. He sways slightly as if to say, "I'm here, not there."

He looks me longingly in the eye and gently asks, "Are you ready for a kiss, or is it too soon?" My heart is racing. I'm nervous about the public space, about the kiss, about everything. I say nothing, but my eyes say everything.

He leans in for our first kiss, which allows me to feel his passion pulse through. It's the first time I've kissed someone since my marriage ended. I'm sucked in deep, way over my head, thinking crazy thoughts: *Oh my gosh, this guy is incredible, I'm going to marry him! What a coincidence, the first man that I meet is perfect. We're going to be together forever! I'm in love again!*

It's amusing how quickly I jump to those conclusions, and it goes to show how deeply the desire for a monogamous relationship is ingrained in my life. After fourteen years spent with one man, it just made complete sense that this was the one—or the *next* one, at least. I wasn't foolish enough to express my instant attachment to him on that first night, but it appeared as though Michael was just as into me as I was into him. While nothing sexual happened between us that night, he was scheduled to stay in Austin for a few more days, during which time we continued seeing each other as often as possible. It turned into a long weekend date. Our friends were thrilled that we had connected so well and that they'd fulfilled their duties as matchmakers.

Michael returned to Dallas midweek, but we kept in touch, and he soon invited me up to visit him the following weekend. It all happened so fast, this whirlwind new romance. While staying at his place in Dallas, one thing led to another, and soon I was having sex with someone other than my ex-husband. I am not sure Michael was completely on the same page. Although there was a lot of passion between us, I was the one who aggressively pursued sex. I recall his comment to me was, "Are we seriously going to do this?," Not exactly how that moment had played out in my mind. It was fulfilling, but immensely awkward.

Even the idea of discussing sex had become difficult for me, much less how to express it. When Michael gently inquired about my sexual fantasies, I couldn't answer him, in part because I wasn't comfortable, but also because I didn't *know*. This was another piece of me, another desire that needed to be rediscovered. It had been so long since I had allowed myself to actually want something, let alone explore it.

Cracks began appearing right before my eyes. After spending so long in a monogamous relationship, sex had become a duty and something to be bartered with. If I couldn't show up, be my authentic self and communicate my needs and desires in the bedroom, then it just wasn't going to work with Michael—or with any other man, for that matter.

This was also evident outside of the bedroom, when Michael would ask me a straightforward get-to-know-you type of question, such as the styles of music I liked. Crazy as it sounds, I couldn't answer this one, either. I didn't have my own feelings or thoughts about music, or books, or TV shows, because my identity had been subsumed by marriage for so long that I was almost too shy or fearful to share those likes and dislikes with someone else. I'd lost my voice in my last relationship, to the point where it was difficult for me to show myself and be able to say, "This is who I am, and this is what I want." I sought the guidance of a therapist who attempted to guide me out of the fog by suggesting that I be "present and mindful." I heard what she was saying, but I didn't fully understand what that meant. I was shut down and unable to connect with my own thoughts. I felt like a hollow shell of my usual spunky self. Plainly, I needed work.

Michael was patient, engaging, and active as a lover, and he continued to suck me in. I ate up his attention, intimacy, and affection, but a few days later, he had a trip to Siberia planned. This sounds like a flimsy and intentionally mysterious excuse that someone might use to flee an unwanted situation—*I'll see you in a few weeks, honey, I just need to visit Siberia!*—but this trip had been booked months in advance.

Michael is insanely passionate about exploring the world and helping others in need. His empathy runs deep, and it isn't uncommon for him to do things such as sponsor college education for several deserving Europeans. He seems to thrive on helping others achieve success. He often tells me his greatest dream is "to maximize human potential and minimize human suffering." He's always working on behalf of the less-fortunate, which might turn out to be a problem for us, as I'm not a wounded bird with a broken wing.

Of course, Michael had no phone or internet coverage while in that remote part of the world, so I spent the next two-and-a-half weeks consumed by low-level anxiety as I thought about our fledgling relationship and how badly I wanted it to work out.

✻ ✻ ✻

Although Michael never married, his last relationship had lasted ten years, so he was highly attuned to the emotional turmoil that I had been experiencing since my divorce. I think my forthrightness scared him a little. He'd say to me, "Look, I'm the first person that you've dated in a long time. I think you're projecting and need to give this some space, to think things through." He would then push me away creating a virtual distance between us. Once he returned from Siberia, I half-expected our mutual infatuation to continue from where we left off. I saw him again in Dallas, but it was awkward between us now, and the more awkward it became, the more anxious I became. As a result, I scrambled harder and harder to try to make it work with him.

One of the paradoxes of intimate relationships is that sometimes, the faster you run after someone, the greater the distance between you becomes. This was certainly the case with Michael, who returned to Europe for business, while I continued to try conducting a long-distance relationship. After a month or two of coping, trying to manage my affection for someone I couldn't physically touch, he put an end to us. He called one afternoon, and I couldn't help but press the idea that I wanted him to come home. "You have been gone for weeks, and it's starting to feel as though I am not important enough," I said. "It's difficult for me to compete with your passion for helping others. It makes me feel selfish, but I need you here."

For a long moment, he was quiet. Then he spoke in a slow, soft tone. "Look Kelly, I have been behaving as if you are my girlfriend," he said. "But you are not my girlfriend. I care for you deeply. We have an unbelievable bond. I've never tried so hard to be respectful, understanding, and not to fuck something up, but you are making this too difficult."

I sat on the hardwood floor where I was just standing and tears began to well in my eyes. I knew where this is going.

"This isn't working," he continued. "We're broken and you're trying to piece this together. It just isn't going to happen. I don't know what to say, but sometimes it is like you aren't even there. I'm having a hard time getting to..."

There was an uncomfortable silence. He took a deep breath. "I feel you have a lot to sort out for yourself. I just don't want to be caught up in this." While he said that, my mind was scrambling to determine what I could possibly say to pull him back to me. I knew he was right. I hadn't said all the things I wanted to say to him. But I couldn't speak.

He sensed that I was holding back the tears and filled the awkward silence by trying to reassure me. "You are an incredible woman," he said. "Once you get settled, you will be able to date whoever you like. The world will be your oyster. You are poised to live your life in such a fulfilling way. Do what you need to do to get yourself back on track."

I could say nothing to this. All I could think was that I wanted to date him, and he was denying me the opportunity to connect with someone in a real way. Why couldn't he be a little more patient? I eked out some words from my feeble voice. "Just a little more time?" I asked. He was slow to respond. "Kelly, I need to go now," he said. "Take care of yourself in the way that you know how."

His words crushed me. I was devastated, especially considering that tremendous connection I felt and the strong feeling that we were going to be together forever. I couldn't understand how he was refusing that connection, because I know he felt it, too—at least at first. As painful as it was to be rejected by him, my emotional response made it quite clear just how much work I had to do on myself before I could return my self-esteem and self-confidence to anything resembling normal levels.

Looking back, I feel as though I was frozen in a state of denial for much of the 14 years I was married, but I tended to see the best side of any situation and kept moving forward. I had become robotic in my nature, going through the motions of trying to make my husband happy by doing what I thought a wife was supposed to do: cooking, social engagements, school functions, rinse, lather, repeat. I was disconnected from my true self and my own wants, and the worst part is that I didn't even know it until after the fact.

As a wife, what I feared most was the loss of a relationship. When that worst fear came to pass, I felt that loss deeply and painfully, but in time I realized that it wasn't quite as bad as I had feared. I like to compare this feeling to skiing, where you're afraid of falling, so you choose the easiest paths in order to minimize the risk of feeling pain. But everyone falls eventually, and when you do, often you realize that the pain isn't as acute as the horrific, limb-loosening crash that you had imagined. It's not the end of the world. You pick yourself up, choose a new path, and continue down the mountain— now an even better skier.

The truth of the matter is that marriage is hard at the best of times. Even attempting to divide a relationship into columns clearly marked 'good' or 'bad' is a tricky task in itself, and no one ever seems to want to stop and say to themselves, "My gosh, my marriage is in the shitter right now. Maybe I need to take a look at myself and make some adjustments." Instead, I think most of us—women especially—tend to keep marching on down the path, trying to hold it all together and keep the peace.

It's this sort of toxic thought pattern, I've realized, that can contribute to irreconcilable differences in a marriage. Women are particularly bad at putting ourselves first: usually, the children come first, followed by the husband, then the career, and we're stuck in fourth place. It's ironic, because we tell strange stories to ourselves, like "I'm going to get a manicure every two weeks to take care of myself." I've been as guilty of this as anyone else. Hell, there's a multi-billion-dollar industry that exists purely to make women feel better about themselves, if only for a moment, whether it's nails, fashion or cosmetics. It can appear as though you're performing self-care, but often it's only at a purely aesthetic level. We're not *really* caring for ourselves by putting ourselves—our needs and our wants—first.

I should be clear: I'm not discounting this sort of behavior. I think it's a beautiful and essential thing for a woman to take pride in her appearance, and to have a lot of respect for herself in every way. Nails, fashion, and cosmetics can all play into that self-identity. But we often ignore the much harder work of actually stopping to think about yourself and what you want, and being able to articulate that to those closest to you. It's about having a voice, and standing up for you first and foremost, and it's something that I think many women miss. I sure did. I don't care which Ivy League school you went to, or what kind of high-powered career you may have: any woman, anywhere, can lose her true self to the desire to please a spouse. Once you've lost yourself, it can be extremely difficult to rediscover.

Funnily enough, during the year that my husband I tried to salvage our marriage, I dropped my fear of loss and began vocalizing my likes and dislikes to him. I became stronger in the midst of a failing marriage. I saw that I needed to continue down that path of finding what I needed and wanted. I learned that this is something I had to do on my own. And so I began to do just that.

Two

LIVING IT UP IN THE HAMPTONS

"I met an old lady once, almost a hundred years old, and she told me, 'There are only two questions that human beings have ever fought over, all through history. How much do you love me? And Who's in charge?'"

ELIZABETH GILBERT, EAT, PRAY, LOVE

I wake up at the tail end of a six-hour flight as the airplane touches down at JFK Airport,. I'm groggy, having spent the night before at the opening day of the annual Del Mar horse races in San Diego. It was a great time, involving lots of champagne, ponies, and big hats—but I was paying for my sins today, having stayed up too late. Perhaps it is the time in my life, but I'm giving myself full permission to live it up... *somewhat* fearlessly.

While at the racetrack, I met a professional paintballer

named Oliver. I didn't know that such a vivacious career actually existed, but apparently it does. Afterwards, I couldn't help but research this profession. As it turns out, Oliver is one of the few in America to earn a decent living from firing paint at other grown men. I was somewhat relieved to know that if I was with a professional paintballer, at least he was one of the best in the world.

Intriguing as discussing paintball was, I knew this was not my future. He called it an early night because he was heading to Amsterdam in the morning for a tournament. As the plane taxied toward the terminal, I realized that my time spent getting to know Oliver was probably a waste. How much could a professional paintballer contribute to the life of a divorcee with four kids? I wasn't sure, and I didn't want to find out. While walking off the plane, I resolved that I needed to start putting some structure around the questions of who I am and what I'm looking for, rather than just waiting for opportunities to present themselves to me.

A close friend from Austin, Jenny, is waiting at the airport in our town car. Equal parts intelligent and beautiful, Jenny dominates the Texas boys' world of oil and gas. She has been single for a while, so her sense of realism about our respective situations is appreciated by an amateur like myself. Unlike me, she understands the game. While she believes in love and in taking a chance, she's always that voice in the back of my head encouraging me to stop and think about the truth of a situation. When I'm in doubt, she's a great sounding board for ideas, inclined as she is to tell it to me straight.

Our destination for the weekend is the lavish and luminous Hamptons on Long Island. The town car heads east as we travel toward the town of South Hampton, complaining about the traffic, looking at the quaint towns that line the beltway in Long Island, and wondering whether we should have taken the train that runs from JFK. We're staying with another Austin friend of ours, Whitney, who is a successful news and media personality. However, her true life's calling is matchmaking. Whitney is also the author of *The Man Plan*, and was previously Match.com's relationship expert; she is well-known for her dating advice and ability to introduce kindred souls. Spending time in the company of these two women—Jenny's realism crossed with Whitney's outgoing, bubbly personality—always makes for an interesting combination, especially on a girls' weekend like this.

Jenny and I take a quick look around Main Street, and then it's straight into girl time. For some reason, when girls get together, it's just like reverting to being in college again. The routines of giggly conversations, borrowing items of clothing from one another, and recommending accessories are much the same, despite the time that has passed. It is so uplifting.

Getting ready for a night out alone is one thing; doing it with your girlfriends is almost dreamy, as we get swept up in feeling good about ourselves. It makes me feel younger, as it's a chance to step outside of the daily routine. Any time I'm surrounded by strong, powerful women who have good things to say about each other, I find that it's a great mutual booster. Honesty is prized above all else in these situations, because if one of us were to head out looking like a fool, the others would have to claim at least partial responsibility. Before we leave the house, it's speak now, or forever hold your peace.

We take Whitney's vintage Ford Bronco, which she has

affectionately named Woody, to dinner at a quaint restaurant called Little Red. As we dine on mussels and chicken paillard, we catch up on dating, travel, and careers. After a sumptuous dinner we are eager to move to the next spot. When we slide into the Bronco, we discover that Woody is tired and does not want to start. Whitney would never let such a minor detail deter our fun, so she begins working on plan B.

The distance is short, so we are considering walking or hitchhiking to the next venue when our waiter exits the restaurant. He offers us a lift to our next destination, the Southampton Social Club. We take a look at the car and note he has three baby seats locked in the back row. We glance at each other to see if we agree to do this. Simultaneously, we lunge into the compact Kia and do our best to squeeze our butts into the tiny Graco seats. He drives us the eight or so blocks, and we are extremely grateful for this beautiful gesture from a guy who's just worked a 12-hour shift, and who I'm sure should be getting home to his young children.

The Southampton Social Club is a white-table restaurant during the day, but at around 10.00 pm they take away the furniture, and it becomes a pumping bar and dance floor. There's a DJ, a beautiful lawn including a garden, and a fire pit. It's one of the most popular spots in town, so there is quite a line to get in. Whitney takes one look at the queue and isn't having it: 5'10" and statuesque, with long, blond hair, she confidently strides up to the bouncer in her heels and begins flattering him, smiling coyly and asking whether he remembers her from last year. He eats it up, of course, and we're let right in. I'm amazed: this is the kind of social engineering trick that I'd never be able to pull off. I'm the type of person who tends to wait at the back of the line, hoping that one of my friends has the balls to do it.

I'm last in the door and hesitant as I take in all of the singles mingling at the bar. I take two steps inside and a guy walks right in front of me. He's tall, broad-shouldered, and looks to be in his late 40s or early 50s, but he's strikingly handsome. He stops and says, "Don't I know you from somewhere?"

It's so sudden that I'm caught off-guard. I'm still so fresh in the dating game that I'm just gullible enough to wonder whether he could be right. I cock my head to the right and take in his features. He *does* look a little familiar; I catch myself thinking perhaps I've seen him on TV. I quickly snap out of it and tell myself that he's trying a bullshit line on me, and that I should just dismiss him and keep walking.

Whitney has the exact same thought and begins helping me try to take care of this unwanted intrusion. She doesn't want the first guy that sees us to get his claws into me, so she shoos him away. We grab a drink and head out to the back lawn, where, sure enough, the same guy reappears and makes a second pass. "So are you from New York, or do you live here?" he asks. My jaw drops, thinking to myself, are you fucking serious? Am I that unremarkable? He doesn't realize that he hit on me like two seconds ago? Is his game *that bad?*

Of course, Whitney calls him on his bullshit right away. She starts busting his balls about his terrible approach, but I guess it's a successful icebreaker on his behalf, as he's now chatting to us. He picks up that Whitney lives in Manhattan, so they fall into a discussion about neighborhoods, restaurants, and social scenes. One of the great things about her supreme matchmaking skills is that she knows exactly which questions to ask up front, so that within five minutes, we know all of the qualifying details about this guy's life that I could possibly want before deciding whether he's worth my time. He's single—divorced with grown children—and seems quite successful: he went to law school, and he owns a lucrative hedge fund in Manhattan.

This all spills out of him during a short but effective—and somewhat combative—conversation. He's a true New Yorker, direct and abrupt in his language. As he bristles at the sharpness of Whitney's queries, I feel as though I'm watching two wild rams butt horns on the Nature Channel. These two strong personalities clash against each other until, soon enough, Whitney eases off and gives the proverbial thumbs up that he may proceed to talk to her friend. Through all of this, I'm sipping a Paloma, loving her strength and admiring the fact that this man is confident enough to withstand her brusqueness.

My divorce was only finalized three months ago, and I'm still nursing my wounds and bruises from my humbling experience with Michael, so I'm not exactly firing on all cylinders this weekend. I know that I want to date again, and I know a little more about what I'm looking for, but my expectations for this trip are purely to have fun with my friends. This is my first venture to the Hamptons, and I'm just looking forward to getting to know the area while meeting new people. The last thing I want is a time commitment to someone I just met in a bar.

However, Timothy seems to align better with the men that I've recently been bumping into: he's age-appropriate, he's a father, and he's undeniably handsome. The fact that he lives in New York City isn't exactly logistically desirable in the long-term, but I reason with myself that since this is just a fun weekend in the Hamptons, I have nothing to lose. While we sit together by the fire pit, I find that I'm able to have a deeper conversation with him than yesterday's talk of paintball tournaments and Amsterdam.

Working in finance, he has developed a highly opinionated style of communicating. This is underlined when I begin talking about my life in Texas and my young family. Without hesitation, he replies, "Oh, well I don't date women with young children." That hurts. I snap back, "Okay, well nice chatting with you," expecting our conversation to end. Yet we continue talking by the fire pit long into the night. I come to admire his directness and honesty: he knows exactly what he wants and what he doesn't want, and he's not afraid to make either of these things known. I desire that. I desire truth, honesty, and someone who can communicate. Sitting outside in the sea air, watching Whitney and Jenny flinging their hair around and dropping it on the dance floor I'm overwhelmed with joy. I'm sucked in by Timothy and savoring this moment.

Eventually, it's late, and he asks if I want to come back to his house. I hesitate. This whole concept is still so foreign to me—meeting someone at a bar and going home with them—so I nervously ask Jenny for her thoughts. I'm attracted to him, so I kind of want to take him up on the offer, but I'm not confident enough to say yes. She's unsure, too, so she walks back to him and asks for his full name. He answers, but follows up with a caveat: "Don't Google me, because you could find a lot of unflattering things about me, and I don't want you to look at that without me around to explain." Jenny smirks and gives me a side-eye, which says, "It is up to you."

As we leave together, I see Jenny mouthing to me, "Oh,

I'm soooo going to fucking Google him!" You can't say something like that in the company of strangers and expect them to withhold their curiosity. We get a taxi back to his house, and since it's already incredibly late, we end up falling asleep together after some kissing and pillow talk. When I wake up, just as the sun is rising, I'm in a house overlooking the North Sea Harbor. It's a beautiful, serene view, yet I'm freaking out a little because I have no idea where I am. I don't know much about Timothy, yet I decided to leave the bar with him—with someone who actually said, "Don't Google me." What if he is an axe murderer? What the hell, Kelly?

My only thought in this moment is that I have to get out of here. My rustling around near the bed for my possessions causes Timothy to stir, and as he groggily asks what I'm doing, I tell him that I'm ready to go back to Whitney's. I'm about to book an Uber when he stops me. "Absolutely not," he says. "I'm going to take care of you. I want to take you home." It's an awkward morning-after conversation. I'm looking forward to the thought of being in a private car, alone with my thoughts.

On the drive back, he offers to stop for coffee and extend our time together. I decline as I'm exhausted and not into it. I slyly glance at my phone to see if I've missed anything from the night before. I see a message from Jenny: "Did you Google him yet?" I want to answer immediately and let her know I am ok but I can't because he's sitting right next to me.

After a short ride down the country roads, we reach the town, and he drops me off with a kiss. I quietly creep back into Whitney's house for a few hours of sleep. When I wake, it's not even 9.00 am and my phone is full of messages from him, asking about my plans for the day, and where we'll be having dinner together tonight. I'm torn: part of me is happy to hear from him so soon, and the other part feels as though it's all too much, too soon. This is meant to be a weekend away with my girlfriends, and now this is complicating matters.

I head downstairs for some coffee and breakfast, and Jenny can't wait to speak with me. Wide-eyed, she's got a big grin on her face, but of course she doesn't say anything: she wants to hear my side of the story first. Which, naturally, is Pollyannaish: I choose to see him as a sweet guy who has been divorced and who's having a hard time building a new relationship. He's gotten a bad rap, he's a darling. On and on I go, until Jenny pulls up the New York gossip website *Page Six* on her phone, revealing his nasty break-up where huge dollars are at stake. There are allegations that I can't even continue reading; it seems acrimonious on both sides. My coffee cools on the bench beside me as I read, enthralled but also crestfallen to learn of these complications. We sit in silence and marvel at the classic Hamptons pool and lush back yard.

Jenny, the voice of reason, says, "I don't know whether this stuff is true or not, but I don't think this is somebody you should be hanging out with." She has a point, but I can't stop myself from replying, "But something about him is so seductive." Listening to my heart leads me to believe that he's a good guy, just a bit misunderstood. Still, I can't shake this news report from my mind, and I decide to keep my distance from him. His text messages continue pinging into my inbox throughout the day, so I finally provide a response, "We will see each other again. Trust me."

He responds well to this directness of decision, and seems

to appreciate my firm tone. It's almost as though I'm holding up a mirror to reflect his assertiveness. These are all small lessons in the bigger goal of knowing what I want, setting boundaries around those desires, and learning to communicate with strength. I'm still very much like a baby fawn finding its legs in this regard, especially since Timothy is so forceful. Yet his directness works against him somewhat, as I don't feel so bad about pushing back strongly and stating my needs with the same kind of clarity he constantly shows me.

Late on Saturday night, we briefly meet at another Southampton club. Again, I'm taken aback by his statuesque presence and his alpha male strength. He gets right to the point by asking about my plans. "Jenny and I are going back to New York City for a couple of days to hang out with some friends, but we have nothing scheduled," I reply. Instantly, he responds with an offer. "I would like to drive you back to the city," he says. "I have plenty of room at my apartment. You and Jenny can have your own room, so there is no need to get a hotel." He sweetens the pot by suggesting that he take us out to dinner tomorrow night. What a gentleman! I'm bowled over by this offer, but I know better than to accept immediately, so I defer the decision until I'm back at Whitney's house.

Jenny points out that riding with him would be more ideal than taking a town car. Whitney holds up her hand and says, "He's going to take you out to dinner—ask him which restaurant he has in mind." Again with the brilliant qualifications! It's a smart call, so I text him back: "Jenny and I will ride back with you. Where do you want to have dinner, so we can plan appropriately?" He responds that he already has reservations for the three of us at Jean-Georges and Carbone. Whitney raises her eyebrows. "I don't know," she says, "Those are the two of the most difficult reservations to get in Manhattan right now. So you should go, if for no other reason than to see if he actually has the reservations." Meeting adjourned.

Timothy arrives at Whitney's house at midday on Sunday. He lifts our luggage into his SUV and is polite to Whitney, even after the sparks that flew during their first run-in a few nights earlier. I'm in the front seat, Jenny's in the back. His driving is making me nervous as hell: he's just as aggressive in the car as he is with his speech. All the while, he charms us with his stories. It turns out that the Escalade is a rental; he wrecked his Mercedes when he rear-ended someone on the beltway. I grip my chair, revealing white knuckles, while making a mental note to never let my children ride in the car with him.

Our conversation turns to Jenny's business, which leads Timothy to offer bold and unsolicited—but not unwelcome— advice on how to be more cutthroat in how she operates. He's telling her exactly what she needs to do, and to not take no for an answer. Sitting quietly, I again admire his decisiveness, and marvel at how successful men in his position can take a small piece of information and combine that with their intuition, experience, and judgment in order to make a swift decision. It seems that once Timothy has his mind made up about matters, there's no changing it.

This forthright attitude extends to dating advice as well. Jenny tells Timothy about a guy who she has been having a hard time reconnecting with, which prompts him to offer some astute observations of what is most likely going on in this guy's head. I can't help but notice that he has strong insights into the heart of the problem between Jenny and her estranged lover. His terse delivery is pissing Jenny off, especially as it's hard for her to hear. He's right, but he can't articulate his advice in a softer way to make it easier for her to stomach.

I'm thriving on all of this, however, as I have recently spent time being around men who have a hard time communicating what they want. They either choose to outright lie, to not speak the truth, or to sugar-coat things to minimize any adverse reactions. I'm attracted to Timothy because he has the rare ability to say what's on his mind without stopping to consider how the other party might react. He's an asshole, basically, but his direct manner is a breath of fresh air to me. This even extends to his rented car: he could have pretended that it's his regular car, opting not to tell us about his wrecked Mercedes, but it's simply not in his character to hide something like that.

The two-hour trip passes quickly, as Timothy is a great tour guide, regularly pointing out landmarks and telling stories. The Hamptons are notorious for attracting terrible traffic on the weekends, but his expertise means that he knows every back road to take in order to get out of there as efficiently as possible. He decides that we'll eat at Jean-Georges, as it's closest to his home. The impression he exudes is one of getting exactly what he wants, every time. It's alluring to the point of intoxication. It'd take a strong person to match him.

I ponder the fact that he already had two dinner reservations for Sunday night. I suppose it shows that he likes to plan several steps ahead. I wasn't easy or agreeable to his attempts to make arrangements, but rather than being upset or getting aggressive, he just moved forward with separating me from my friends. He must have thought to himself, "Oh, I'll bring her back to New York." That Jenny was with me was no impediment, either. It all seems to be in service to a master plan, which doesn't have to happen immediately. He's patient.

We arrive at his building, 15 Central Park West. The building is an opulent white tower made of modern cut limestone. We pass through a stately bronze door at the west-side entrance and take the elevator up to his apartment above the trees, which looks out over views of the park from the southwest corner. It feels like I'm in a castle. I'm mesmerized by the sheer greenness and quiet of it all. We're floating above the chaos of New York. It's dreamy. Jenny and I trade glances, barely containing how impressed we are. Timothy shows us to our separate guest rooms, where we prepare for dinner a few blocks away.

We opt to dine outside on the summer evening. All through dinner, Timothy is highly engaged with Jenny, making her feel comfortable and getting to know the both of us better. He's a perfect gentleman, and my attraction to him only increases as I spend more time with him. Our night ends with a short kiss, and since he has work the next morning, Jenny and I are left to rise at a more leisurely time and visit the MOMA. As Jenny and I browse the various floors of art, we review the weekend and the haste of my new connection. I'm smitten by him, and confess as much to Jenny, who smiles and listens patiently, before pointing out that he seems very controlling. I can't deny that, but I'm intrigued by the question of where I might fit into his master plan.

Timothy made it clear to me that he was looking for a

companion for the summer, and what began as a random weekend meeting in the Hamptons turned into a whole summer of weekend vacations while long-distance dating. I found myself becoming a New York commuter: whenever I didn't have the kids, I'd usually leave on a Thursday to meet him in New York or the Hamptons. He took care of travel details, from the flights to the driver, often going so far as to arrange my ground transportation in Austin. As an independent woman, I had to ease into feeling comfortable with letting go and allowing somebody to care for me.

Our clash for control was sometimes taken to ridiculous extremes, like on my first trip back to visit him in New York. He was texting me things like, "Baby, are you at the airport yet?" I'd reply dutifully, and he'd type, "Okay good. I just wanted to make sure you had enough time and you weren't late for your flight." Five minutes later. "Baby, you're going to land at terminal 4 and my driver, Derek, is going to pick you up. Make sure you go to the second curb." Every detail of my trip was micromanaged from thousands of miles away. I thought to myself: doesn't this powerful man have a company to run? Why is he concerning himself with whether or not I'm at the airport? I text Jenny, who assures me this is an endearing quality. She jokes, "Baby, are you alive?," trying to help me make light of the situation. I laugh and relax a little.

Although Timothy is endearing, I can't shake my agitation or the feeling that he is treating me like a child. I've traveled the world; I'm in my 40s, I have four children, and I'm fully capable of getting to a fucking plane on time. Why are we even having this conversation? It felt juvenile, and I was wrestling with my urge to speak up and tell him so. At the same time, though, I was trying to become comfortable with this new situation of being taken care of, down to the most minor details.

On this particular trip back, I landed at a different terminal at JFK than the one he'd anticipated, so his driver Derek was nowhere to be found. I quickly made the decision to grab an Uber instead. When Timothy found out, he hit the roof. You'd think it was the end of the world. He was *furious*; he bombarded my phone with messages, saying it wasn't safe and that he didn't know which route I was taking.

When I got to his apartment, he was just finishing up a workout with his personal trainer, which I was grateful for as it probably allowed him to blow off some steam. Just as he was about to forcefully exert his authority, I sternly said to him, "You know what? I made that choice. It was the right one, so just leave it." And to my surprise—and his credit—he did. He smiled and nodded, and agreed that I'm a capable person who can make her own decisions. I was exuberant. I made a choice and used my voice. It was a small victory, but a significant one.

During that first Sunday night at Timothy's with Jenny, I had some of my perfume and beauty products laid out in the guest bathroom. When I next visited him, I was surprised to find that he had replicated my products, which were laid out just as they had been the first time. He was extremely attentive, also stocking the house with my favorite Quest bars and breakfast items. I wrestled with his consideration. Why was I so uncomfortable being taken care of?

Clearly, he wanted me to feel comfortable there, so that his home is like my home. He'd said as much, multiple times, and had even given me a key and ensured that the doorman knew me. It felt like I was just a cog in the wheel of his bigger plan. Whether the plan was to have a companion for the summer or for life, I wasn't quite sure. He wants to share his life with someone, and his wealth means that that life happens to be full of fabulous things. He's used to dating Manhattan women and models who more or less demand to be taken care of, so when I didn't adhere to that expectation, he was a little thrown.

* * *

One summer afternoon in the Hamptons, Timothy and I are relaxing on the beach at Gurneys' resort in Montauk, sipping a bottle of Domaines Ott rosé. Timothy checks his blackberry and monitors stocks as I leisurely watch the staff rearrange the beach and lounge beds for the sunset party. I'm enjoying our relaxed intimacy when suddenly, my past life comes peering through the proverbial curtains. For the first time in months, I receive a text from Michael. The last I'd heard from him was that he was dating a 25 year-old Californian girl who he claimed to be madly in love with. Michael says that he has landed in Austin because his flight to Dallas was diverted. He was thinking of me while he was grounded, triggering a long text conversation that sets my heart racing.

The smartest thing for me to do in this situation is to tell him that I'm with somebody right now and can't talk. But despite myself, I can't put the phone down. I can't tear myself away from this opportunity to reconnect with Michael, a man who I felt so strongly toward for a time. He begins questioning me about why I was in the Hamptons; these queries are friendly, but veer into judgmental territory when he says, "It sounds like you're dating somebody with a lot of money. I didn't think you'd go for someone like that." Our dialogue has an antagonistic edge to it that I really don't need or appreciate. This is supposed to be a romantic, developmental weekend for me and Timothy, yet here I am, allowing Michael to not only invade that space, but, once I took the conversational bait, my mind as well. Eventually, I tell him that I have to go, but the damage is done.

Later that evening, Timothy and I dine at The Crow's Nest, taking in a romantic sunset. Timothy is reviewing our wine options, but I'm preoccupied, thinking about Michael and what went wrong between us, replaying scenes and wishing I could press an 'undo' button. I want to know why he was thinking of me. He had just returned from a trip with his girlfriend; why was I on his mind and why was he texting me? What did that mean, and what should I do? These are silly, unanswerable questions, but I can't shake them. Timothy notices my preoccupation, but I don't tell him what's on my mind. Part of me wants to open up to him and tell him about my conflicting thoughts. How could I? None of it made sense to me. I didn't feel affirmed by Michael's attention, only judged.

As time went on, I realized that other than the simple desire for companionship, I was also looking for security in a relationship. This word can mean a lot of different things to people; I'm not even one hundred percent sure I know what it means to me. A lot of women believe that marriage is a guaranteed lock-in as far as security is concerned. Even now, I have friends who say, "Don't you want to get remarried so you'll never be alone?" My response is generally to look them in the eye and tell the truth: even in marriage, there's no guarantee that you're never going to be alone. A ring on your finger doesn't necessarily equate to security. So what does security truly mean?

Timothy, for a lot of women, is the very picture of secure. I admire him from across the candlelit table. He exudes confidence. He has money, power, control and the ability to make things happen for himself and anyone else around him. He's the archetypal Prince Charming in that sense. Is this my Prince Charming? Does he embody the security that I have dreamed of for so long? I can't deny that I am seduced by the thought he has the power to rescue me in some way.

Timothy was unbelievably kind and patient with me as he helped me make sense of my divorce. Sometimes it was as though he understood elements of my marriage better than I did. He supported me, and wouldn't tolerate my thoughts of self-blame or shame. His kind words and patience gave me space to grow strong again. He constantly reminded me of what a strong, competent mother and woman I was.

That summer exploring Manhattan and the Hamptons was unforgettable. Timothy had given me a whirlwind romance of loving moments and tantalizing parties with high-powered financiers. It was inevitable that we would need to discuss our next steps. This comes to a head one Sunday, as we walk through Central Park, and Timothy broaches the difficult conversation.

"I think that we need to have a plan for the fall, to see how we can take this to the next level," he says. This involves pinning down where we'll spend Thanksgiving and New Year's together. He's throwing around tantalizing and elite destinations such as St Bart's and Anguilla while I'm quietly brewing a minor panic attack.

His seriousness brings a structured view to the future.

I quietly dwell on my personal thoughts of the future and my own complications. I thought that Timothy and I were just going to have fun in the Hamptons for the summer, and then go our separate ways. I never imagined raising my four kids in the city. He senses my concern and begins to paint a picturesque story of our life in Manhattan as we stop on a park bench to listen to David Ippolito, the famous Central Park guitarist.

"Darling, I should let you know I am putting a deposit down on a new apartment in 220 Central Park South," he says, referring to a place better known as the Billionaires' Bunker. "Of course, I'll ensure it is large enough to accommodate the family." I envision the life of an elegant and well cared-for family, living on the Upper West Side. He gazes deep into my eyes trying to get a read on my feeling and suggests we continue to walk. As we near the park's edge he draws my attention to Lincoln Center, where the kids could take music lessons. "There is also a performing arts theater two blocks behind our apartment; perhaps ballet for the girls?" he suggests. "Or equestrian riding lessons in Central Park? The list of resources for our family would be endless."

I have to admit that, in the moment, I buy into the dream a little. I've spent so much time in his neighborhood that it's starting to feel like home. He's done such an impactful job of making me feel comfortable at his apartment, and in the area, that I feel torn. As we leave, we decide to stop at The Smith for a late lunch. We have some wine and dine alfresco, watching native New Yorkers wind down their weekend. It's been an invigorating day so far, and I have the undeniable feeling that I'm living this lovely dream. It is fraught with complication. I can't deny that I have one foot in this new life as a New Yorker, but the other foot is still in Austin, my true home with my children and my reality. I fear as though I have unintentionally compartmentalized my life. I wonder if I can combine the two new lives of Kelly Green.

It all hits me like a ton of bricks. My eyes swell with tears, overwhelmed by the difficulty of this conflict. It's clear that I'm not ready to make such a big leap. I still feel fragile, and as I tell him I can't do it, I have a deep-seated feeling of remorse. Even as I'm declining his extremely generous offers, I'm wondering whether I'm insane by passing on this opportunity to not only be so loved, but for my kids to have a great education at private schools in New York.

I also feel a sense of pressure, in part because our relationship felt far from organic. It seems as though he has it all planned months in advance, and he's continually looking into the future to see what's in store for us. He has played me into a corner, and I feel that I have to strike out and stick up for myself. In a way, it's quite a departure from our first meeting, when he told me that he didn't date women with young children. He jokes that I'd broken him, this self-proclaimed asshole New Yorker who treats models like shit, who never wants to attach to anyone, and who is very direct about what he wants and doesn't want. Yet in our experience together, he has apparently become a softy who is actually very caring. I think he had blocked that part of his life out after his own children left the nest, and he'd denied himself the beautiful feeling of caring for and loving a family again.

This struggle for power was a huge shift for me to deal with, as I am quite controlling myself. In my marriage, I was the caretaker. My independence and need for control ensured that I was the one who bought all the houses, all the cars, and took care of annoying-but-necessary things like insurance. It was an exhausting way to live life. I didn't allow space in my life for anyone else to do things for me, even something small like book a flight or a driver. Spending time with Timothy throughout those months in New York gave me the opportunity to let go of the need for control, and feel good about being taken care of.

It is a fine line between power and vulnerability.

A powerful man can persuade you to relinquish control and exude feelings of security. You may feel as though you're in a protected relationship. If you aren't mindful, once relenting to the struggle, you can find yourself in a complacent mindset. If someone is making all the decisions for you, you may lose site of what it is you actually want. By the end of the summer, I'd learned that I might have swung too far the other way. I learned that you should have your own thoughts and your own plan for what you want. You don't have to be rigid about it, but if you don't know, you're just going to get sucked into someone else's plan, and someone else's life. I'd already done that in my marriage, and I didn't want to do it again.

Timothy gave me space to voice myself again. It was okay to say what I liked and didn't like. Saying "no" is often honest, and honesty is something most people appreciate. At the same time, he reminded me it was okay to *want* to be taken care of. I will keep that voice with me and never let it go. Yet I knew that I had just begun my journey of healing. I needed to move forward. I knew I wouldn't regret it, and neither would Timothy.

Three

LEARNING TO JUST HAVE FUN AGAIN

"Every woman that finally figured out her worth, has picked up her suitcases of pride and boarded a flight to freedom, which landed in the valley of change."

SHANNON L. ALDER

Some mornings, waking up alone in Austin is too much for me to bear. There are times when I wish I had someone to take care of me, even doing something simple, like bringing me coffee in bed. In the morning haze, my mind drifts, and I consider that it'll probably be another nine or ten years before my eldest child can drive to Starbucks for me. My eyes snap open when I realize—who am I kidding? A teenager is never going to drive to Starbucks for me. That's insanity.

My eldest son has seemingly read my mind, when he comes into my room and asks, "Mommy, can I bring you coffee?" I feel like he has sensed my loneliness in that moment and intuitively knows what I need from him. I give him a hug and a kiss, and remember how truly blessed I am to have these small moments with these beautiful little people who care for me so much. I know that I can get wrapped up in thinking about men, dating, and my romantic future, but moments like this reinforce just how much I receive from them.

I recently purchased a Nespresso machine, which is worth every penny. It's so well-designed and easy to use that my 7-year-old can drop in a pod, warm up my almond milk, and then bring me a perfect almond cappuccino, which starts my day off just right: full of love.

I sip my coffee and realize I'm running late for the day. My ex-husband is on his way over to stay in-home with the kids for the weekend. During our divorce process, we both decided to put our grievances aside and put the children first. Our youngest son was still in a crib, and we mutually agreed that minimal disruption to the children and their schedule was vital to their stability. For the first year after the divorce, we agreed to a 'nesting' arrangement. Nesting is a family law term that conjures sweet, lofty notions of little birds floating around an ethereal nest. The reality of nesting is that it is really fucking hard on the parents, but provides balance for the children.

They were able to digest what divorce means on their own time, not ours. Piece by piece, they understood the terms and impacts of the changes, yet still had the stability of their dedicated parents. As for me, I had to leave the nest every other weekend, in search of a place to perch. This created a sense of urgency for me to find something to do and somewhere to be. Fortunately, my girlfriends were always happy to support me in this exhausting endeavor. This weekend, I am off to Los Angeles.

I have a friend I met at Coachella a few years ago named Mila, who's celebrating her birthday. She's from Belarus, and this is her first visit to the City of Angels. We are both euphoric about the weekend. I can't wait to share the experience with her. I love Los Angeles, as there's a part of me that has always felt at home there. In a way, it's my happy place, but at the same time, it has a devilish, soul-sucking sort of vibe. While visiting, I'm always struck by the city's bizarre contrasts. The weather's so consistently perfect, but at the same time, everyone's very clearly out for something. They are continually trying to get ahead in ways that are more transparent than in any other city. Trying to be better, look better, sleep with more attractive people, improve their careers—or all of those at the same time. I can see why people portray it as superficial, but if you can get past that, it's a beautiful place. I am particularly excited to be residing at the Chateau Marmont, set high on a hill above Sunset Boulevard. Every inch of the historic hotel has a story to tell. In particular, the lobby's red carpet and cathedral-like windows evoke an 'old Hollywood' feeling that suggests mystery, glamour, and scandal.

I arrive early; my room is not quite ready. I decide to make the most of it and head for the sunshine. I search for a chair as I canvass the oval-shaped pool, which is surrounded by red-and-white-striped umbrellas. The landscaping is full of lush vegetation and ivy lining the fence. I find a chair and sink in, closing my eyes to feel the warmth of the August sun mixed with the California sea air. The pool is sparse in the early afternoon. I notice a couple of people who are covered in tattoos and appear to be nursing bad hangovers shambling around in slow-motion, like ghosts of actual humans. I leisurely glance around and notice a man at the bar who fascinates me. Laid out before him is an extremely elaborate tea set, with agave, raw sugar, Stevia, and various tealeaves. It gives the impression that he's a high-maintenance kind of guy, as there's a lot going on over there, and he appears to be very particular in his tastes.

Even from a short distance, I can sense his high energy and his intensity. It scares me in a way that I can't quite put my finger on; my intuition tells me that I should stay away from this person. Yet I'm so entranced that I can't take my eyes off him. He has his swimsuit on, his shirt off, and his body is just flawless. Every single muscle is well-defined, and he's wearing a long necklace with a crystal pendant. His skin is perfect. His face reminds me of Tom Ford, with an impeccably groomed beard. He exudes a style that's attractive and captivating, with a touch of arrogance. I'm trying not to look at him, but of course I'm side-eyeing him, mesmerized.

I don't want to give him the satisfaction of knowing, however. As he comes my way, I do my best to make sure that I'm looking elsewhere. I overhear him saying something about how he's intending to go trail running in the canyon; it sounds fierce. I haven't been this nervous around a man in quite a long time. He has a pure physical presence that intimidates me, frankly. As he walks by, he doesn't say anything. He doesn't even look at me—not even a side glance. Part of me is relieved, but I'm wearing what I thought was a sexy new L*Space bikini, so I'm feeling pretty good about myself. I'm not sure what I would have said if he did make eye contact, but I'm also disappointed that there isn't any reaction whatsoever.

As he walks off, my eyes trailing his tail, a couple of my weekend companions arrive at the pool where we greet each other with hugs and kisses. I quickly dismiss the thought of the handsome unknown and remind myself there are plenty of fish in the sea. Mila arrives and we excitedly review our weekend plans full of untold adventure in La La Land.

Throughout the weekend, I occasionally pass him in the hallway of the hotel, or while having breakfast in the courtyard. We share some eye contact and smiles, but no words are spoken until the final day of my visit. Mila is flying back to San Francisco, and I've elected to stay an extra night with my friends in nearby Pacific Palisades. On this Sunday morning, I'm now one of those people who is nursing a hangover by the hotel pool. I glance over at the empty chair next to mine, and notice a newspaper and a pair of sunglasses. Just as I'm processing this, up walks the mysterious tea-drinker, who sits down beside me.

I can't stop staring at his body. I'm extremely nervous, but he's warm, engaging and friendly. We begin chatting about how we spent our respective weekends, and over the course of the hour I learn his name, Alex Smith—which he spells out for me, almost as if he wants me to Google him. He lives in London while running his alternative investment company based in Paris. He's also a key figure in the art world, including a spot on the board of a prominent art museum. I mention that I'm staying at a friend's place in the Palisades tonight; he replies that he's going to a party on the beach, and suggests that we meet at the Nobu in Malibu for dinner. My heart is racing as he says these words, and I can't think straight enough to commit. He seems to sense my discombobulation—perhaps my hangover is a contributing factor—and offers me his number, suggesting that I can text him if I think I'll make it to Nobu.

After he bids me farewell, I instantly Google him and discover that it all seems to check out—the museum website is one of the first results. I decide that I should take this risk to spend more time with a fascinating, dazzling man. He certainly gives off an aura of living a fabulous life, and I could see myself happily becoming a part of it. Having learned from my most recent dating interactions, I didn't reveal much about myself in that first encounter, a decision influenced by Timothy's strong reaction when I told him about my four children. I recoil a bit at that memory. I'd become a little gun-shy about sharing my personal information so soon after meeting a stranger, and Alex seemed happy enough to satiate my curiosity about him.

I relax in the sun and recall his dinner invitation, thinking it was certainly forward. But because he has a boyish quality about him—clearly confident, but also a little giggly and excitable, which I relish—I wasn't quite sure if he was approaching me as a friend in L.A., or whether he was eyeing me as a potential dating candidate. He certainly wasn't as assertive as Timothy. It felt adventurous and unknown. In that moment, we were just two people hanging out poolside at the Chateau Marmont. Who knows where we'll go from here?

After making sure that I saved Alex's number in my phone, I head to Pacific Palisades, where I reunite with my friends Dennis and Kimberly. They've been very supportive throughout the divorce, and they're both excited to hear that

I've begun dating again, though Dennis is highly skeptical about me meeting some guy at the hotel and accepting a dinner invitation. He reminds me of a concerned parent, but his excitement for me wins out. I think they—like me—are hopeful for my future.

Alex arrives at Nobu wearing a black cashmere sweater, which is the single most luxurious clothing item I've ever seen on a man. I learn that it is an Italian brand, Loro Piana, and it's quite exquisite. He greets me with a kiss on the cheek, and throughout the course of our sushi dinner, the jovial quirkiness of his personality starts to come out. Most notably, I learn that he doesn't eat or drink very much. As we make our dinner selection, I request the Rock Shrimp Tempura. He looks at me as though I have two heads, and says, "You do realize that one is fried?" His hand glides on my thigh "Let's stick with the yellow-tail sashimi." Halfway through our meal, I realize that I'm eating way more than he is. I begin to wonder if I can hang out with a man who eats less than I do. His discipline is likely the key to his flawless physique. The conversation shifts to me. He's enamored by the fact that I'm a Texan who drinks tequila, and he seems to find the simplicity of my life and my tastes endearing. The way he articulates this is genuine, not condescending, so I don't take offense.

Over dinner, we become more acquainted and begin covering some of the basics. He grew up in New York and was educated at Harvard and Oxford. At this, I cower; I'm reluctant to tell him I went to Texas Tech, wondering if he even knows where Lubbock is. After college, he had immense success on Wall Street and eventually moved to Europe to conquer the world of global finance. As a result, he runs in an interesting international social circle. He has an aristo-cratic feel about him, and we're mutually fascinated by the contrast of each other, since we've experienced such differ-ent upbringings and lives. Our bodies lean in, ignoring the outside noise and distraction of the restaurant. We get along fabulously, becoming fast friends.

Alex begins to come alive as he expresses his passion for art. I watch his body language as he tells a story about his favorite chair, which was created by the famous German artist Rolf Sachs. It was a collector's piece on its own, but Alex is bold and took it a step further and had Dutch art designer Maarten Baas "singe" the chair, to create his infa-mous char-grilled furniture. I'm taken aback by his calculated creativity. I could barely keep up with what he was describing. I imagine his apartment in London and conjure up a scene of the Sachs-Baas chair and my children sitting on it with their pudding fingers. I giggle at the thought of meshing my chaos with his pristine life.

We've spent several hours talking and dining at the bar. We decide to move to the deck at Nobu; he's had half a glass of red wine, and I'm on my third tequila. It's still not clear whether this is a date or the beginning of a friendship. As we stand near the wooden rail, listening to the shallow waves, Alex answers that unspoken question by kissing me. It is dark now, and the ocean is slightly glowing with the lights of Nobu. It's incredibly romantic, and I adore the feeling of being swept up in fascination with this new man.

Alex suggests that we continue the evening at the Chateau Marmont, where we have a great time laughing, people-watching, and poking fun at celebrities. We find a sofa and cuddle under the comfort of a heat lamp as he playfully whispers in my ear speaking part French and part English. I begrudgingly check my phone and notice that it's 3.30am. I take a deep breath to subside my sudden panic. Reality kicks in; I have a 6:00 am flight home to Austin. I've got 20 minutes to get back to the Palisades to pick up my bags, and then to the airport in order to make the flight. I regret that I have to hurriedly say goodbye to Alex. As we kiss, I'm reminded of our contrasting worlds and that he lives in another country. Our lives are complicated and busy. I cherish the last moments together and think that I will probably never see him again.

I arrive in the Palisades to a beautiful, Spanish-style California home that was once owned by Diane Keaton. I make my way though the heavy wooden gate and head to the front door. It's locked. Of course it's locked, because who the hell leaves their house unlocked in order to cater to the needs of house guests who have chosen to stay out way later than they should have?

I pace around the driveway guilting myself. Why do I always have to push my fun just a *little* too far? I can't ring the doorbell and wake their children. I think of Kimberly's beautiful twins and their perfect blond hair and big blue eyes. I imagine them sleeping peacefully in their big, comfy beds. Perhaps I could call or text Kimberly? I quickly dismiss that idea; it takes her three hours to answer a text on a good day.

I remember a side door that connects to the pool. I stride toward the darkness of the high hedges that have been growing for several years. These are the kind of hedges that can only be found in Los Angeles: perfectly manicured and 15 feet high, providing privacy from the famous Sunset Boulevard. I sense their proud history and feel protected by their whimsical strength. I approach the door and hold my breath, turning the knob. No luck. I make my way to the backyard to calculate my next move.

The grass is dewy from the morning ocean air. I pass the lawn chairs and note that I may be sleeping there for a few hours. I imagine myself hung-over and cold from the moisture, waking in pain as the morning sun rises. I visualize a troublesome scene of being found as the children let the dogs out. Ah ha! The dogs!

I remember a doggie door in the butler's pantry, connecting to the kitchen. While dashing to the other side of the house my adrenaline rushes, I now feel like a burglar. This could be considered breaking and entering. I size up the dog door. It is small—*really* small—but it is my last hope and I decide to try it anyway.

I've managed to get half of my body through the dog door. My shoulders and head have cleared the square space. However, I've miscalculated my body size and can't seem to squeeze past my waist. I'm stuck; body half way through. In my haste and struggle to gain entry, I haven't noticed that Kimberly's three dogs are sitting directly to the left of my head. Their oldest and largest bull dog, Batman, is particularly interested in my antics. I am in a very compromising position to have three dogs staring at me. My chest is tilted down toward the floor, and my ass is up in the air on the other side of the door. Will the dogs bite me? Will they bark?

I slow down to pause, holding my breath trying to appear as small as possible. We all take a moment and stare at each other. I speak softly and reintroduce myself. I hope they remember me. The younger two dogs are bored and unimpressed with my early morning disturbance. They turn, sauntering out of the kitchen and back to their beds. Batman diligently remains. He lets out a long sigh, as only an old bulldog can. I look at him and I feel as though I see empathy in his eyes. He is rather large; perhaps he, too, has been stuck in this very position. He probably knows exactly how I feel. Or perhaps I am just the biggest dumbass loser he has ever seen. The failure of my master plan is beginning to sink in. I heave a big sigh and lay my head on the kitchen's cold Spanish tiles. What am I doing? Shouldn't I just be at home, in bed, asleep? Did I need to meet a stranger at Nobu? I turn to Batman, who is still waiting patiently for me to sort out my life. His breath is slow and labored with a small amount of drool coming out of his mouth. He looks up behind me with such intent it is as if someone is there. An angel? The nanny? I struggle to turn and look up behind me. I see nothing, but he exudes determination and is still staring. He is looking at the doorknob! Yes, he's right. I can reach it. I swiftly wiggle around and unlock the door, swinging it open and dragging my suspended body with it.

I can't believe it. Freedom! I pull myself out of the door and rush to grab my bag. Batman is still in the same spot. I take a moment to give him a big hug and kiss. He hasn't moved an inch since it all started, but he seems very pleased with himself. I make a mental note to speak to Kimberly about her canine home security system and Batman's keen ability to assist late-night intruders. My phone vibrates with a message: "Your Uber is arriving." Just in time. I take time to pause for one last moment before I return home to reality. Batman. My hero. Until next time, my love.

* * *

Alex lives in London and his life is so full, but a month later, I receive a text from him. He tells me that he'll be in New York next week for his birthday party at a new private club called OMAR'S. "It's a distinguished crowd," he wrote. "It'll be incredibly chic. You should join us!" My instinct is to say "Yes!" immediately, as I had such a fun time with him, but I'm unsure about the nature of the invitation. Am I being invited as a friend? Should I bring a date? I've only spent around 12 hours with this guy. Is it a little crazy for me to be flying to New York for the birthday party of a man I barely know?

I survey my New York friends for opinions, asking whether they've heard of OMAR'S. The response is unanimous: it's an awesome private club, and I should go. I ask Whitney to accompany me, but she'll be on a flight to Paris. Generously, though, she offers to let me stay at her apartment. This seals the deal for me: I'll go to his party, my adventurous side wining and spinning out of control. I book my flight and cherish my newfound freedom.

Spending time in New York reminds me of my tender time with Timothy. Feeling wistful, I decide to text him and let him know I'll be in town for a birthday dinner. He has said on several occasions that we're friends, and that he'll do anything for me, so when I tell him that I'm heading to New York, he invites me to stop by Jean-Georges for a cocktail. He has a charity event booked for the night of Alex's birthday, so it all seems quite reasonable and agreeable. The planets are aligned.

After I land at JFK, it's a shit-show as usual getting into the city, so I'm running late for our cocktail. Timothy texts that he's just finishing up his workout, and diverts our plans at Jean-Georges to his place for a glass of wine. Instinctively,

I realize that it's not a great idea, as it'll throw my already disrupted plans further out of sync, but how can I resist visiting his apartment and that view again?

When I arrive, Robert, the doorman, greets me with familiarity and a side wink, "Good evening, Ms. Green." The suggestion is very clear and I'm tempted to shout at him, "We're *just* friends—can't we just have a drink?!" But I realize I'm wheeling my luggage behind me, so it sure as hell *looks* like I'm here to stay. I purse my lips and head up to his apartment.

The view still takes my breath away, and I'm filled with a sense of nostalgia, as though I'm returning home after a long vacation. There's an easy sense of familiarity that I've come to associate with Timothy's apartment. He greets me at the door with a glass of DuMOL pinot noir—my favorite, and quite hard to find—and shows me to the guest room where I've stayed previously. "Here's your room back!" he says with a devious, but warm grin. He toasts our reunion.

I recognize that calculated smile—it is the expression of a man whose plan is falling into place! We were supposed to be having a drink out, but here I am, back at this beautiful apartment, catching up on our respective lives. He's very honest about his dating life, and tells me that I opened him up to trying new things. He shares how he shifted his dating focus and he's not dating the same types of women he'd previously been attached to. He credits our time together, and he says that he's highly appreciative of our relationship and how it changed him, which is sweet and intimate. I can't help but notice the growth and wisdom since I've met him.

I'm captivated by our conversation and haven't been watching the time, so I'm running late to prepare for dinner at Whitney's.

Timothy smiles and says, "Baby, you know you're not going to make it down to Soho in time..."

Here it comes, the master planner in action. I have to concede that he has a point: there isn't enough time. His suggestion is for me to stay in the guest room; he'll leave me a key, and I can come and go as I please. I accept his generous yet contrived offer. When Timothy reemerges from his room, he's wearing an Ermenegildo Zegna custom suit, giving him an air of being at once regal and confident.

With a peck on the cheek, he bids me farewell, and says, "Have a nice evening, darling. I won't see you in the morning, because I'm going to be leaving for work early and I don't want to wake you." He drops a key in my hand, folding my fingers over tightly and kissing my hand. "The apartment's yours. Enjoy the rest of the wine. Call me the next time you are in New York." I'm a little overwhelmed by his generosity. I spend some time reflecting on Timothy as I drink the rest of the pinot while overlooking Central Park. He is a fascinating man, and I'm glad that we get along so well, but my mind is distracted and filling with questions about my looming evening and where things sit with Alex. Am I party filler, a friend, or something more?

To calm my nerves, I remind myself of how fun he is. Even though I'm going into this adventure completely alone, I trust that it will be a good time. I walk into OMAR'S, wearing black Louboutin booties, a pink layered chiffon Chanel skirt, and a navy blue military jacket. I'm a little late by my standards, but I'm still the second party to arrive, which just goes to show that New Yorkers tend to be ridiculously late to their social engagements. The first couple I meet is an odd one: he's an elderly Jewish gentleman in his 70s, and she is a beautiful Japanese woman who's wrapped in fur and dripping with enormous diamonds. After I introduce myself, I learn that she's an art dealer—one of Alex's good friends—and she's wearing jewelry provided by her escort, who's a diamond dealer.

As the guests start trickling in, I notice that they're almost all European, with names like Svetlana, Francesca, and Sophie. They're extremely chic and clearly embedded in this international world that I am not. I'm feeling very out of place and nervous, until finally Alex arrives and gives me the standard European double air-kiss. There's no physical contact, though, and therefore no indication of whether or not I'm his date. After more introductions and cocktails, he breaks the awkwardness by coming over to me and rearranging the seats at the birthday table so I am next to him. He's still surrounded by six women, so I can't be sure if he's genuinely interested. I begin to feel as though I'm starring in an episode of *The Bachelor*. I wonder if there'll be a rose ceremony.

The woman to his left is named Sophie. She is drop-dead gorgeous, with high, pointy cheekbones, soft blue eyes, and perfect just-fucked hair. She begins making efforts to stake her claim on him by putting her hands on his chest and speaking French to him. I sulk; I cannot complete. I don't speak any foreign languages, which certainly makes me a fish out of water: everyone here seems to be bilingual as a minimum qualification. Sophie has the gall to ask me to take a photo of her and Alex, which seems like a move clearly designed to piss me off. Rather than giving her that satisfaction, though, I simply take the photo and move my attention away from her and onto those sitting nearby.

The woman to my left engages me by inquiring what I do, and when I tell her that I work in technology, she appears bored by that mundane answer, so I don't elaborate any further. When I ask what she does, I learn that she's a meditator: she shuttles around New York, running major group meditations, all day long. I'm thinking to myself, "Is that free? Or something one can get paid for?" That concept is as foreign to me as these people.

It's only when the table realizes that I'm not from another country that they ask where I live. When I say the magic word—*Texas*—all of their ears prick up. They think it's the most astonishing thing ever that I'm from Texas. It's as though I'm a bizarre, exotic animal that they've never seen in the wild before. I'm overrun with questions about Texas, tumbleweeds, tequila, and myself, and then banal statements about how they always fly coast-to-coast, never opting to land in my home state.

The overwhelming impression of those sitting at the table is something like, "Oh Alex, she's so *darling*." I'm bemused by this condescending tone, as if they're talking about a Chia Pet or something, but I take it in stride as I warm up to the crowd and their interest in me. After dinner, we transfer to the bar, where everyone's socializing amid enormous silver balloons that trail long strings toward the floor.

Champagne is being passed around when, finally, Alex grabs my hand, whisks me into a coat closet, and plants a huge kiss on me. His hands are slowly sliding up my fluffy skirt, and there is heavy groping between us. My legs are loosely wrapped around him, and our hands wander all over each other. We've gone from zero to a hundred in mere seconds. I embrace every bit of it, right up until the snooty manager opens the door and tells us with a disapproving scowl etched on her face that Alex needs to come out of the closet, because it's time for his birthday cake.

Alex is glowing as his three-tiered fondant cake is wheeled over to him. He closes his eyes as if to summon a big wish and studiously blows out his candles. I wonder if he will eat even a bite of the sumptuous cake. The crowd begins to thin. A smaller group of us decide to continue the evening with after-dinner cocktails. We arrive at The Boom Boom Room, a lavish lounge on top of the Standard Hotel. It's known for its breathtaking skyline views, gorgeous interior, and a strict guest list after 11:00 pm. After taking our table, one of Alex's party guests, a concert pianist from London, plays some brilliant music while we gather close and bask in the moment. I'm feeling great; my role with Alex is secure, and I'm interested to see where all that groping might lead.

While enjoying this unforgettable New York moment, however, my phone vibrates in my purse. It's a text from Timothy: "Baby, it's late. Why aren't you home yet?" I had forgotten all about Timothy, and the fact that my belongings were sitting in his apartment. Oh, shit. Is this really happening? I quickly tap out a response, telling him that dinner didn't start until 9.30 pm.

His reply: "What did I do to make you not love me?"

Oh, *no, no, no*. Not now, please. I've had way too much wine, and I'm having way too much fun to possibly deal with this deep and complex issue right now. I realize that I'm suddenly homeless and need to sort out sleeping arrangements. I can't go back to his place to retrieve my belongings; it is now very awkward. I tell him that I'll stay at Whitney's instead. Our brief exchange has put a damper on the night, and now it's starting to infect my mind.

It's late, and the crowd at The Boom Boom Room is breaking anyway. Before Sophia leaves, I make sure to ask her to take a quick photo of Alex and me on my phone. She does not take it well but reluctantly snaps the photo. I suppose she does not like the end of this particular episode of *The Bachelor*. After all, only one girl can get the rose. As Alex is saying his final goodbyes to his friends, I sneak into an Uber, ready to head down to Whitney's. I settle in and direct the driver to Spring Street. I'm startled when the back door swings open. Alex quickly jumps in, placing his hands around my waist.

He kisses me on the cheek "Salute, babe," he says, a phrase which he uses at the beginning of all of his greetings. He says he needs a ride, and as the driver accelerates, he asks me to come back to his hotel for a nightcap. I smile, but I do not respond. Alex confidently takes control and tells the driver, "To the Pierre Hotel".

The Pierre is an old-school, English style hotel located on 5th Avenue, the Upper East Side of Central Park. With its gold details and wall murals, it feels rather stuffy after a posh evening of nightclubs. While leading me through the quiet lobby at 4:00 am, the tall, thin night manager dips his glasses to take a closer look. One awkward elevator ride later, we find ourselves at a door marked The Hutton Suite. He stops to kiss me as he simultaneously slides the key in the door. He kisses me passionately as his hands become entangled in my hair. We are a webbed mess as we stumble into the door, arms and legs intertwined. Although we have chemistry, I sense a respectful boundary that lets me know this is fun, but as far as it will go. We continue to kiss awhile and it all stays fairly innocent until we fall asleep. Three hours later, his phone is buzzing with work messages, and I wake up fuzzy from lack of sleep. While stretching, I look out the window to a beautiful view of what would be a gorgeous fall day if not for the heavy fog that shrouds Central Park. On a sunny day, I would be able to see across the park directly into Timothy's apartment at 15 Central Park West, but not today. To complicate matters, I have a conference call scheduled this morning and my laptop is sitting in that very apartment. If only I could flap my arms and soar from balcony to balcony.

Somehow, despite snatching just as much sleep as I did, Alex already seems to be operating at full capacity, dressed in the hotel's plush white robe; he chats with his PA about meetings, future travel arrangements, and today's schedule. Despite how little he seems to eat or drink, his energy is enviable even at 6:00 am. I, on the other hand, have barely opened my eyes: I'm half-dressed, my bra is on, my skirt is all askew, and as I'm getting my bearings, he hands me the breakfast menu and says, "Here, babe. Just order one of everything; I'll have the garnish on your plate from whatever you get." We share a laugh over this, as we both know it's true. He coolly turns his attention back to his assistant and the work at hand.

When I'd queried him about his tiny appetite earlier, he told me that it's part of his disciplined, regimented approach to life. It feeds into his appreciation for art and all things beautiful: he wants everything to look a certain way aesthetically. His restraint in eating and drinking is just another way for him to maintain control over himself and his life. It's fucking insane, which he freely admits, but I respect his dedication. When the food arrives, he samples his cappuccino, and it's not warm enough. He makes a joke about it, but I can tell it bothers him, and if I wasn't here, I'm pretty sure that he'd make a complaint and order some appropriately hot milk.

We eat breakfast together—well, I eat, he drinks his almond milk—and it's nice, but I'm still not sure how I feel about him. We're friendly, and I'm obviously drawn to him and the way he lives within an international circle of fascinating people.

"What was the last girl that you dated like?" I ask.

He is somewhat slow to respond.

"Darling, I am very cautious about who I become involved with. I generally don't pursue women because I don't want to find myself in a situation that is difficult to get out of."

I respect his caution and wisdom. Perhaps I should temper my "say yes" attitude with a bit of his scrutiny. I can't help but wonder if I am passing the test as I survey my multi-plate breakfast while looking down to brush out my crinkled skirt and mis-buttoned blouse.

Alex also shares that he is in the process of finalizing his divorce, and it clicks for me that we are in the same spot of self-discovery. He, too, is loving his newfound freedom and is eager to see what life has in store for him. He tells me that he travels to study people, to understand a country's finance market and see and understand how people live and work. It's a highly stimulating, informed, and intriguing way of seeing and thinking about the world, and I lap up the conversation, as it's far removed from the usual types of things I hear Texas men talking about. I can learn a lot from Alex. I'm enthralled with our conversation and surprisingly pleased at how well get along so well. I don't want to the morning to end.

While lost in conversation, I temporarily forget that I've got a conference call scheduled for 9:00 am. It's inching toward that time, which of course means that the surrounding streets are stuck in the gridlock of rush hour traffic. As I'm gathering myself to leave, I glance over to see that Alex is disappointed.

"Darling, is it really necessary for you to leave for work?" he asks.

The question takes me aback. "Yes, it is," I reply. "My job is important"

He's trying to convince me that this call isn't worth the hassle, but I know better: I don't want to let my clients down, and hell, this is my career we're talking about. I've worked hard for it, and it's extremely important to me, not least because it helps me to support four small children who rely on me. I try to explain this to Alex in as few words as possible before kissing him goodbye and heading downstairs.

I've got less than 20 minutes to get across Central Park, but first, I have to make the walk of shame through the crisp lobby of The Pierre. I am very clearly wearing my outfit from the night before; my once-smoky eyes are now looking a little worse for wear. I'm avoiding eye contact with all of the clean, buttoned-up guests, looking like a complete ragamuffin as I stomp toward the door. I check my Uber. He hasn't moved in the last ten minutes. Ron, my driver, is stuck in traffic two blocks away, and I'm distraught so I risk my Uber rating and press the cancel button. I collect my thoughts and make my way across 5th Avenue to the park, which I know well by now. I can almost hear Timothy's voice guiding me to a shortcut. I spot a pedi-cab driver who sees how frantic I am, but as I run toward him, I glance in my handbag to discover I have zero cash. He quickly understands and offers to take me across for free. A free ride in Manhattan—I must look desperate!

In my haste, I have a moment of clarity as the fog in the park begins to lift and make way for the beautiful yellow and orange fall foliage. In my panicked state, I can't help but be struck by a genuine feeling of good fortune. I feel incredibly lucky to be standing in this beautiful field on such a gorgeous fall day.

No other moment than this one matters to me. Although I feel the distant pressure of work and daily tasks, I push it aside. The colors around me become unusually crisp and I feel the fall air as if it is a part of my skin. It is almost as if time is suspended. I am suspended in this moment. It dawns on me, amongst the city traffic and chaos of my life, that *this* is what it feels like to be present. A window has opened for me.

Something in me clicks; I know exactly what I need to do. I start running, in this outrageous outfit and stiletto booties, as the clock nears 9:00 am on a Friday morning. I feel free and vivacious as I run from one man's hotel room to another man's apartment. It's a surreal scene as I trek the mile or so across the park from irresponsibility to responsibility, keeping my appointment. Tourists are gawking at me, intrigued and snapping photos. Little do they know that they are capturing me feeling more alive than I have in years.

F o u r

THE ROCK STAR

"Darling, my attitude is 'fuck it'; I'm doing everything with everyone."

FREDDIE MERCURY, 1979

That last visit to New York was incredibly invigorating. As ridiculous as it might sound, that silly moment of running through Central Park in stilettos set me on a course of positively embracing change and chasing the unfamiliar. Confidence began flooding back into my life, and it fueled my momentum. I'd passed the newborn fawn stage and could now walk on my own, which is just what I'm doing a few weekends later when I attend the Austin City Limits music festival. It's held on two consecutive weekends in October in Zilker Park, a 350-acre green expanse in the heart of the city's south. This year, it's being headlined by Eminem, Pearl Jam, Outkast, and Skrillex, but rather than cramming in as much music as possible—which is exactly what I would have been doing a couple of decades earlier—I'm there to see old friends and meet new ones.

On the Sunday night of the first weekend, I've secured a pass for the closing party in the artists' lounge, a gorgeous space beneath huge oak trees lit by globe string-lights and populated with picnic tables, food, drink stalls, and people of all sorts. There's a great vibe going on as the festival winds down. Most of the artists in attendance have already performed earlier, so they are primed for a long night of celebrating.

I've spent the weekend bouncing among different friends, enjoying their company without becoming attached to any one group. In the artists' lounge, I'm sitting with Emma, a married friend who grew up in Paraguay. As a result, she's got a lot of that South American spitfire attitude; she's very vivacious, direct, and fun to be around.

While we gossip over a drink, a couple of hipster-looking young guys come over and sit with us. As we get to know them, it emerges that they're both single. Although I'm gaining newfound confidence, I am not prepared for flirting with two men at once. I'm overwhelmed with the signals I'm receiving from both. By now, though, I'm wise enough to understand that yes, they are both interested. Eventually, one of them moves to sit down next to me. It looks like that decision was made for me. I turn my head, and before I know it we are kissing.

As the festival winds down, my newfound love asks if I'd like to go somewhere with him. I think, *where is somewhere?* I know that we can't go back to my place where there's a nanny and four kids, which probably isn't all that attractive to a hottie like this. When he suggests that I can come with "us," I don't even know who "us" is, or where I'm going, but feeling adventurous, I accept his offer. Emma is moderately concerned for my safety and well-being and decides to come along, if only to keep an eye on me. In the company of Noelle Scaggs, a singer-songwriter from the band Fitz and the Tantrums, we all pile into a white van, which drives us to the other side of the park. When we step out, we're confronted with the sight of a large maroon tour bus.

There's no way I'm going to get on a musicians' bus. It seems like a cliché that's just not worth fulfilling. I question my judgment of picking up a musician roadie. But some chatter in the van regarding the band and their performance leads me to realize that the two guys from the picnic table are members of Phantogram, an electronic rock act who I'd seen—and enjoyed—on stage earlier in the weekend. With their credibility established, my hard edges soften, and I get on the bus. To my surprise, it's incredibly nice. It's quite spacious inside, with a communal living room area that leads to a series of four sets of bunk beds. At the back, there's another, smaller living room that can be closed off with an accordion-style door. I could actually imagine enjoying living here while touring the country—with the right company, of course.

I snap to my senses when I realize that there's only one other girl on this bus—Emma wisely bid me farewell upon seeing the bus. Her last communication was a stern look which told me to be careful—nine guys. It's quite possible that I've bitten off more than I can chew. This is exactly the type of thing I will warn and forbid my daughters against doing. Thankfully, these guys are all incredibly sweet and friendly and quite clearly comfortable in one others' company.

I suppose you would have to be, living in such close quarters for months at a time. It's beautiful to see how close their friendships are, particularly between Josh—Phantogram's singer/producer—and his supporting group. I observe their interactions and immediately connect with Josh's depth and loyalty.

Their warmth eases my nerves, and as we settle into conversation, I learn Josh and Chris live in Brooklyn and New Jersey, respectively. Meanwhile, the bus is trundling down the road, and I have no idea where we're going. Nicholas is the guitarist who kissed me at the picnic table, and we head to the back room together. As we make out for a little while, the bumpy dirt road and swaying bus makes it difficult for our lips to stay connected. We're soon interrupted as Josh abruptly slides open the accordion door and glares at me.

He give us a sly smile. "What's going on back here?" he asks, even though the answer to his question is obvious. He's acting strangely, and not giving us any privacy, and it's at that moment that the bus pulls up at the Holiday Inn in East Austin off Interstate 35.

To be clear, this is not somewhere I'd ever choose to go, in Austin or anywhere. A few weeks ago, I'd been living it up at the Pierre and 15 Central Park West; now, it appears, I'm slumming it in a Holiday Inn. As the bus comes to a stop, and like clockwork, the band and their road crew are rolling out some of their gear and luggage; it's clear they've done this a few times. I'm in awe of their on-the-road routine as they strip their bunkbeds and unload their uniformly bulky luggage. We make our way to the lobby where I fidget uncomfortably, waiting while they check in.

Nicholas and I are in search of some privacy, curious to

see where tonight might go. He grabs his hotel key and my hand. Josh is still being awkward about it, like he's never seen two people attracted to each other. He and Chris head out for a drink, but the awkwardness and transition has broken a bit of the spell between Nicholas and me.

Now that we're alone, Nicholas begins roaming around the room, seeking something that's buried in a pile of luggage. Finally, he pulls out a large camera. It looks expensive. I sense that it is precious to him, and that he's protective of it. I realize at that moment that we are complete strangers. He knows absolutely nothing about me. I giggle as I get the sense he thinks I might steal the camera. He glances over at me. I smile at the thought and try to reassure him I have no interest in his silly camera, only him.

He comments that he hasn't eaten all day and that he'd like to take a shower. I suppose most musicians are probably pretty dirty and sweaty the majority of their lives. After all, who has time for a shower at a music festival, and where would you take one, anyway? Dirty musicians on a tour bus: it feels dangerous and I kind of like it.

I lay on the cushy bed of the Holiday Inn, taking in my surroundings. After staring up at the popcorn celling, I turn on my side placing my hands in a prayer position under my cheek. I watch him undress. It's quite nice, watching a 30-year-old shower. I take in the moment as I enjoy how decadent it is: that ass, those abs. I'm happy to be transported back to my younger years. Looking around the room, I once again find myself outside of my normally comfortable, predictable life.

It's another moment of stunning self-realization. What am I doing at a Holiday Inn on the east side of Austin with a complete stranger? This is a far cry from luxurious Manhattan. Perhaps I should make a break for it and sneak out while he's in the shower. After all, why am I here? Have I completely lost my mind? If nothing else, it is indeed awkward.

My thoughts drift back to the tour bus and how quickly I was willing to just jump on it and go to an unknown destination. At 42, I should know better. Nicholas steps out of the shower. He senses my hesitation.

As he wraps the towel around his taut waist, he gives me a tender look, and says, "You know, you can leave if you like. I don't want you to leave, but you are free to go if you want to."

This small act of mutual acknowledgment that I have a choice allows me to relax and remember that I chose to be here. I made that choice only because it's fun, and it makes me feel good. Perhaps this isn't what my therapist had in mind, but I'm exhilarated by the risk of the situation. I know what I want, and I'm not worried about what will become of this. I decide to stop the self-shame and judgement of my decision. Fuck it—what do I have to lose?

Too few hours later, I wake up face down, fully clothed in my own bed. My Monday morning alarm seems to be set at a higher volume than usual. I snooze and wonder if I will regret my decision to keep things on an innocent level with Nicholas. I don't think it's likely that I'll be making out with a young, hipster guitarist anytime in the near future. I snap to my senses; all the right choices were made. It was lovely, but he does live on a tour bus.

It's a school day for the kids, and I'm rushing to get them ready while clouded in a hungover, underslept daze. As I walk my twins to the bus stop, I see a friend of mine who lives on our street. She's an OB/GYN, looking smart and fresh in her scrubs, and she gives me some severe stink-eye. I'm taken aback to see such a facial expression at this early hour. It prompts me to look down and clock my outfit: the very same dusty Rag & Bone booties, cut-off Daisy Duke shorts and British flag shirt that I was wearing all of yesterday. "Looks like you enjoyed ACL," she says with a smirk. I keep my mouth shut. Clearly, I'm a picture of parental stability, looking as though I've just come out of a mosh pit.

A day later, I'm surprised to see that Nicholas has found me on Instagram. I'm guessing he has nothing better to do while the bus eats up the miles on the road. My blood runs cold when I realize that, by now, he's no doubt seen copious photos of my four kids. My whole story is there: I'm not some fun, fancy-free festival girl, I'm a somewhat responsible adult with my own complex life. Nonetheless, he could have only looked, but I take it as a positive sign that he chose to follow me. We discussed his next show in Dallas, and as fate would have it, I happen to be there on business during the upcoming week.

I decide to take a risk and see the boys perform. It's a Tuesday night concert and I have work the next morning, so I decide to call it an evening when the show ends. As they leave the stage, I leave the venue and head home without speaking a word to anyone. After the show, lying in bed, I try to look at Nicholas's photos and discover that he has blocked me on Instagram. I find it so weird and childish: why would someone go to the trouble of finding me, reaching out, and then blocking me? I didn't do anything to offend him—or so I thought—but his behavior is so annoying that I feel it needs an explanation. I didn't care too much about this interaction to begin with, but now I'm irritated at him for acting like a moody brat. I try to shake it off.

The following weekend, I'm at the second Austin City Limits festival, hanging out in the platinum area, which is right in front of the stage. Watching Phantogram play, I'm so close that I can make eye contact with Nicholas, who looks up twice but doesn't acknowledge me at all. This sucks. My "Oh fuck-it" attitude is coming back to haunt me. I wasn't attached to him, but it's still disappointing to have that connection broken and not know why. My self-doubt begins whispering in my ear: "You're too old. You have kids. You're divorced. Young men aren't interested in you. You're going to be alone for the rest of your life. You shouldn't engage in this sort of behavior, anyway."

It would be easy for me to give in to this kind of negative self-talk. Had it happened earlier in the year, after Michael pushed me away, I'd have been down for the count. Thankfully, my confidence is ascending again. I feel brave and shake Nicholas from my mind so I can continue enjoying the festival. After the music ends, I end up in the artists' lounge again (surprise!), and since it's the second and final weekend, the party is even more intense: plenty of the Austin City Limits staff and organizers are letting their hair down after another successful event. The lounge is packed with a rock-and-roll festival crowd full of leather, exposed skin, and trendy felt hats. I'm enjoying the scene with a group of my Austin friends. Jenny is by my side again, enjoying the night and dancing away under the glow of the festival lights.

We are positioned at the same picnic tables as the previous Sunday. Phantogram is far from my mind, but out of the corner of my eye I see Chris, the band's drummer. I sidle over, and he greets me with the same warmth and friendliness as last weekend. As we take a seat, I have to ask them what's up with Nicholas. Before he can answer, I spot Josh's signature black cap, with the letter 'P' front and center. He joins the conversation and answers before they can. "Oh, Nicholas isn't coming off the bus tonight," he says with a smirk.

I'm confused—he's a responsible adult; can't he make his own decisions? I take some personal offense, and then quickly judge myself for my irrational response. I try and move past my feelings of inadequacy and continue talking to Josh, who looks just as attractive as the first time I met him in this same spot. His face has a boyish quality, which communicates that he's probably somewhat mischievous. He has gorgeous full lips that are difficult to stop staring at. He connects with his eyes as he locks in and focuses on me. Phantogram's performance earlier today demonstrated his enterprising talent and relentless creativity. His musical partner in the band, Sarah Barthel, long ago named him Josh Motherfucking Carter, and rightfully so.

Hovering around the table are several Phantogram groupies who have apparently come all the way from L.A. The girls look almost identical: edgy, young, Bohemian-chic girls who are clinging to his every move. Jenny and Emma gather closer, anticipating the fun that is about to occur. However, Jenny's interest is waning, and she gives me a signal that she is tired and growing impatient with the scene. She excuses herself to go to the bathroom, making a point of saying loudly that we'll be going soon. I reply that I'm ready to go whenever they are. No sooner have I said that than Josh decisively dismisses the bohemian groupies by ordering them to bring him a drink, then swiftly turns back to me, looks me square in the eye, and says "You want to fuck?"

This sends the groupies nutty, protesting that they have traveled so far just to see him. They're screaming at him, and at one another. Jenny rolls her eyes, realizing that her window to use the bathroom has closed as this new dramatic development unfolds.

"Oh no, I am not missing this," she says with a smile.

My mind is a few frames behind what's taking place before my eyes: I thought I was more interested in trying to understand what happened with Nicholas, and now Josh? His hands are hovering near my butt as he turns around, shoos away the four groupies, grabs the back of my head and kisses me. His hands are all up in my hair, creating an irresistibly messy PDA scene. It feels as though the music has suddenly stopped, with that vinyl scratching sound from the movies, and everyone in the vicinity is staring at us.

Of course, nothing of the sort happens: there are people getting physical all around us. It's a fucking music festival, after all, one of the few situations in which public hedonism and expressions of sexuality are tacitly encouraged.

But the way that Josh publicly claims me over the other girls makes me feel so beautiful and youthful.

Who would have ever guessed those four words—"You want to fuck?"—could make a girl feel so beautiful? Those words trigger a monumental shift for me. Unbeknownst to him, Josh has given me a grand gift—I am worthy; I am fuckable! Of course, it's a gift that he has the power to give to many adoring women, but on this night, he chooses to give it to me. I feel beautiful once again, for I am being admired above all other in the vicinity. This may sound superficial, but a man making a woman feel beautiful is extremely important. Although mine came in the form of a direct and terrible line,

I think I was ready to hear it. I believe that if you are listening, a man can make you feel beautiful, no matter what he is saying. If you already know you are worthy, it only takes a slight hint to bring that to surface.

The rest of the night is spent hanging out in the park as the crowds fade away. We walk around, kiss and share jokes. He claims me as his own by putting his arm around me. As people pass by, he shares that we're engaged to be married. It's a fun time, and I'm glad to have Jenny by my side. She's having a similar sort of experience with Chris. As the hour gets late, the band is making plans to head to their bus and onto New Orleans that night, but the boys are both angling to hang out with us for a while longer.

I covertly tell Jenny that Chris is totally into her, and that we should continue our adventure.

"No...he just threw up in the bushes, and I think I'm done here," she replies matter-of-factly. I can always count on her for a reality check.

As we walk slowly through Zilker Park, the workers are diligently tearing down the stages and picking up the trash strewn on the grass. Josh opens up, sharing stories of his childhood in upstate New York and his roots in Brooklyn. Today his life is mostly that of a nomadic gypsy. He takes comfort in his deep friendships and his confidence in his musical talents. His best friend and lead singer in the band, Sarah, has been with him since his early school days. I can tell he enjoys his life on the road, but at the same time, he clearly longs for something more concrete. It seems as though he is searching for his own kind of permanence.

I suppose this is true for everyone. We all try and balance the quest for feeling permanent while wrestling with the uncertainty of the future. Musicians must have a certain amount of faith in the unknown. A calmness and belief in what will be. I can't help but recall my own fears during the divorce as I sat on the edge of a life I didn't recognize. As difficult as it is, it seems joy and creativity can appear when we push ourselves to the edge and patiently wait for threads of the imminent.

Josh's lack of attachment to location appears to allow him to focus on his creativity and be in a flow. I listen intently as he strides across the field, humming a tune between sentences. It is as if I can see a piece of him taking the form of a new song right before my eyes. As we make our way across the field, he pauses to kiss me. His hand slides down my back and into the backside of my jeans. He gives my bare ass a squeeze as he kisses me. I can tell by the look in his eye he hasn't lost sight of his original goal for the night.

I smile, recalling how he desired me above all others. It's a feeling that I will keep deep inside of me. We've almost made our way back to the edge of the park and he is practically glowing as he talks about his upcoming tour and final show in Los Angeles. He is eager to return to creating and recording new music. My mind drifts to my own destiny and my children. I wonder if I could introduce the kids to Josh Motherfucking Carter. Maybe I'd leave out his middle name.

Josh continues his attempted conquest by telling me that I should ride with them through the night, that he'll fly me back home after the New Orleans show. I'm intrigued by this offer, and my mind runs wild with the possibilities. I imagine myself as Kate Hudson's character in *Almost Famous*, but soon enough, I'm brought back to earth with the thought that tomorrow is Monday, and in a few hours I'll be getting the kids ready for school again. Tomorrow, my role at pre-school is 'snack Mom.' I regret that I can't take Josh up on his offer, but I do enjoy reveling in the fantasy. Life on the road: someday, perhaps.

As we approach the bus, Josh greets his manager. While he's occupied in conversation, Jenny and I sneak around the back of the bus, down a dirt path, and along the edge of a lake to quietly sneak out of the festival. We're chatting and laughing at ourselves over what has just happened. I haven't had this much fun since New York. As for Josh and I, there's no goodbye. In my mind, it's to be continued, though exactly when that might happen has yet to be revealed.

Five

THE AIR IN ASPEN

"I'm looking for love. Real love. Ridiculous, inconvenient, consuming, can't-live-without-each-other love."

CARRIE BRADSHAW

Having been on a high throughout much of the second half of 2014, it seemed as though I was due for a reality check. The universe had plans for me: if I wasn't going to press pause myself, then fate would intervene. That's exactly what happened in mid-December, when, striding to get into an Uber, my back foot got caught in a pothole. Surprised to find myself off balance, I fell awkwardly and was met with a world of pain as my kneecap cracked in half.

This was one of those times when I wished that I had a partner, a man in my life full-time, to pick up the pieces and take care of me. One of the advantages of having a great network of girlfriends.is that so many people stepped up and took care of me. Two days after my dumb accident, I awoke to find my Christmas presents were wrapped, my house was clean, and my holiday dinner was ordered. My life was more organized than it had ever been before. I am normally averse to favors and being cared for, but I had no choice in this situation. I had to learn to depend on others, and in this case, I was very grateful for the support and affection shown by my friends.

After a couple of months of recovery, I was getting my life back on track. The break had forced me to slow down and clear my head and my calendar. It unwittingly brought closure to several items in my life that continued to linger. Opening a new chapter, I was looking forward to an adventurous girl's trip to Aspen.

Aspen is often described as a playground for the rich. It is logistically difficult to get to, but even more challenging to leave. Thin air, low visibility, and grounded jets create a breeding ground for brief, torrid affairs. Any given Sunday, the tiny airport bar is filled with new couples reminiscing over one last Bloody Mary before they depart for reality.

The girls and I make the journey from the small Pitkin County airport down Highway 82 toward Aspen, I'm invigorated by the sight of the vast snow-capped mountains. Jenny breaks the silence by telling stories about the men of this town, which Emma dubs "The Legends of Aspen." This is only my second annual venture with the girls, some of whom have been coming to Aspen for nearly a decade. As one, they warn me about the lure of men who live the life of intriguing corporate ventures built on big money and adrenaline-pumping sports. They are described as eternal bachelors that know how to make a woman happy but refuse to settle on just one. Many of the men are repeat offenders, coming to Aspen every year, cheerfully honest about their appreciation of you as a female but never willing to fully commit.

Jenny looks at me with a seriousness that she rarely possesses and says, "They will make you feel beautiful and full of life, but Kelly, you *must* remember, it's only for the weekend. It's just part of Aspen." My heart sinks at the tall tales and the potential for both pleasure and pain. As we near town and pass Aspen Chapel on the right, my eyes soften. This is the church where our host, Emma, and her husband, Marc, were married. I want to remind them all that happily-ever-after can be found in Aspen. That true-love story is sitting right next to me.

Emma sees me eyeing the Chapel and looks at me with a warm smile, as if she knows what I'm thinking, but I decide to keep it to myself. The girls continue to exchange stories like seasoned warriors preparing me for some sort of battle. They're probably right. I try to acknowledge their experience and respect their traditions. As an Aspen rookie, I can't possibly admit that I'm hopeful about my chances, and that perhaps I will find something—or someone—meaningful here after all.

Emma shifts the mood by reviewing this year's planned fun and filling us in on a conversation she had with her husband before she left. Marc inquired, "Why is Kelly going to Aspen with an injured knee? She can't ski." Emma replied that I was going to spend time with my girlfriends and just have fun. Emma says he called bullshit. "No, she isn't," he said. "She's going to Aspen because she wants to get laid."

The car explodes into fits of giggles as I attempt to mount a defense, rejecting the idea that I would have sex with a stranger I'd just met here. Emma continues with the male interpretation of the town.

"Well, let me tell you this," Marc continued. "If she thinks there's long-term potential in a guy, then she probably won't have sex. But if she doesn't care, then she will totally have sex." At this, we all scoff at the male mind.

Our first stop is an Après Ski restaurant called Ajax Tavern. As we walk in, I'm reminded that a sense of unreality permeates the town, as the child-like adults put their regular lives on hold while on the prowl for new experiences. This creates an environment where celebrations, openness, and fun reign supreme, though there's a dark undercurrent to all of this: even the married people seem to be there to flirt, mingle, and have a good time. Not much is taken seriously in such a town. I'm reminded this may be exactly the wrong place to be searching for a long-term partner. I check myself to relax and match the vibe—just have fun.

As Emma and I look around the bar, we joke about the selection of ski-bums contrasted with aging playboys, many of whom the girls recognize from years past. I don't have a clear line of sight, but my attention is diverted to a man positioned by the bar. His back is turned to me, so I can't see his face, but I'm immediately drawn to his physical presence. He has exquisite arms; I can't help but wonder what it would feel like to be wrapped in them. He is balding with a buzz cut and sports a faint grayish 5 o'clock shadow. He has a masculine, rugged, Jason Statham-style look.

Emma follows my gaze and shakes her head. "He's way too old for you," she says. But she would say that: she still thinks that I should be on a musician's tour bus with Josh Motherfucking Carter. I coyly reply that I think he's cute, and she's taken aback. "You *never* say anyone is cute," she says.

She raises two fingers of her right hand, points them at this guy, and motions him over.

Seemingly at the speed of light, he's standing over at our table. It's a little embarrassing how quickly he comes over, actually. None of us know what to say. I'm astounded that Emma did something like that, and also by the fact that it actually worked. It proves to be an effective icebreaker as we laugh about her move and his response, which shows that he has a good sense of humor and doesn't take himself too seriously. We soon pair off, and I learn that he's in Aspen for his 50th birthday. The first stop on his birthday celebration is dinner tonight at Matsuhia, the very same restaurant where my girl-group has an 8 o'clock reservation. We exchange numbers and casually agree that we'll probably wind up running into each other later in the weekend.

His name is Jake, and when I tell him that I have four kids, he doesn't flinch, let alone run for the hills. He also shares that he has a daughter in Los Angeles. I can immediately sense the unspoken bond they share and his deep relationship with her. As we discuss our domestic logistics, I feel a sense of warmth and depth. Although the sexual chemistry is undeniably building, I am struck by a feeling of stability and envision him as a strong father figure.

I am intensely physically attracted to him: I like his age, I like his sense of humor, and I'm drawn to his quiet confidence. He comes across as calm, confident, and efficient. He's a hobby triathlete who's into skiing and biking. Although I've never dated anyone who's super sporty, I find these qualities attractive in him. I contrast these traits against the most recent men I've seen, who will only ride in black cars, collect high art, drink almond milk, or run hedge funds. Jake, on the other hand, feels a lot more grounded and real. He has a genuine substance that piques my curiosity.

I have quickly committed the cardinal sin of putting him in the category of long-term potential. I'm looking forward to seeing more of him and seeing whether we're as compatible as I am projecting us to be. The following night, we meet at the Caribou Club, an infamous private venue downtown. It's a cozy place, with décor that reminds me of a 1980s Ralph Lauren advertisement drenched in tartan and plaid. Caribou boasts a small dance floor and a few separate rooms, one with a fireplace. I am swaying on the dance floor when Jake and I meet again, as our two friend circles collide. We graciously provide some inter-group introductions before Jake takes my hand and leads me to a small sofa nearby the fireplace.

Our conversation is brief, and I feel the butterflies in my stomach growing. We know our time is limited, since we've both committed to activities with our friends. As we make small talk about our respective days, Jake leans closer and places his arm across the sofa, resting his hand on my shoulder. He pauses, and as a gentleman would, asks if he can kiss me. I lean closer towards him, anticipating his touch. It's so electrifying that, to this day, I can't even recall if he is technically a good kisser or not. My whole body is illuminated by his touch alone. Instantly, I want more. He says that he wants to be with me. I feel the same way, but for now, we are both at a loss as to what that means and how it might happen. Reluctantly we separate, but his energy lingers. I can't get him out of my mind.

Later that night, he texts me, eloquently expressing his desire to meet again. Normally, I wouldn't dignify such an obvious booty call with a response, but without hesitation, I invite him to Emma's. It's snowing, and the house in downtown Aspen is difficult to see from the road. I wait for him, watching from the window, anticipating his arrival. Once I see his shadowy figure under the streetlight, I step outside in the cold mountain air and wave as he finds his way across the snow-packed sidewalk. The house is quiet with the other girls fast asleep. We gently whisper as we greet each other with a mischievous smile and a kiss.

I'd told the girls of his potential visit before they went to bed, of course, and Jenny had placed a condom on the living room table. "I'm going to leave this out for you, just in case you need it," she said with a smile. I knew there was no chance of having sex with a guy I'd just met in Aspen, period, but I didn't reject her offer, either.

Jake comes inside and removes his jacket. We make our way into the living room and site side-by-side on the couch. He exudes confidence, but I can't hide my nervous feelings of lust. I am searching for a path to progress beyond our idle talk. I can't help but relish my feelings of how attracted I am to him, diving deep into his dancing blue eyes and the curve of his mouth. He is magnetic and charming, but I'm suddenly struck by a tinge of fear that this is one of the Legends of Aspen that the girls warned me about. Yet for some reason, I don't care. I am completely swept up in the moment, and the thought of getting hurt doesn't bother me at all. I know the uncertainty will be worth the risk. I soften, waiting for him to make the first move. After an awkward pause, the moment consumes us. Our bodies are immediately in sync. Every inch of us melts together as he deliberately eases me onto my back.

Once studiously positioned on top of me, he pauses and

looks at me. "God, you are so fucking gorgeous," he says. His gaze and his words seduce me. His ability to be so close to the moment captivates me. I feel his lower body pressing against mine as he uses his right hand to slightly separate my legs, making space to press himself against me. His hand slides up my back as he gently wraps his fingers in my hair, pulling firmly. He buries his face deep in my neck and hair, his breath quick and aggressive.

Jake swiftly pulls back and readjusts his hand to my collarbone. He stops and looks at me, as if he is marking what is his. He secures his fingers gently around my neck with his thumb, applying slight pressure. Perhaps I should be scared that a mere stranger has me in such a compromising position, but I have no fear, only lust. His movements prove that he is a man and that he is in control, but never forceful. He adjusts to a slower pace as he kisses me softly, checking to see if I am okay with how things are progressing. I relinquish immediately. Physically and mentally, I let go of all my barriers and surrender to my desire.

In this moment, I know that being with Jake will be different than anything I've ever experienced. I don't fight it. I realize I have zero resistance and decide that he can do whatever he wants to me. Normally I would fear that lack of control, but I know that I should simply embrace this chance. I'm unable to resist him, and I don't want to, either: he feels natural and safe. It's almost as if some long-dormant emotion has awoken inside of me, and I'm filled with sexual tension.

I had some good, fulfilling sexual relationships in college, but after being married for ten years, I'd lost my primal appetite for sex. I didn't think about it very often, let alone talk about it with anyone. I had forgotten what I wanted. As Michael found during our first encounter together, I couldn't articulate any sexual fantasies, and though I had some good experiences with Timothy in Manhattan, that part of my life was confined to a dark corner that was largely unexplored. I'd resigned myself to the fact that I was over 40, and that sex just wasn't that interesting anymore. Before the divorce, my husband and I still had sex, but I wasn't present and it wasn't fulfilling. It was as if I didn't know any different. I was going through the motions, a trend which continued until that night on the couch in Aspen with Jake.

Despite our mutual arousal, neither of us is comfortable with the fact that there are eight other girls in the house, and that one of them might walk out at any point. Although I make it clear that we aren't going to have sex on the couch tonight, we both know it'll happen eventually. This knowledge satisfies us both, and after he leaves, I crawl into bed and fall in to a deep sleep. At 5:55 am, I jolt awake, and instantly note that the time on the clock is an angel number: 555 signifies that major changes are about to occur in my life; turbulent, but for the good.

I burrow down in the blankets, feeling the cold, heavy mountain air, I feel tingling in my body while thinking about Jake. I'm sandwiched between two of my best friends, and as I look at Jenny's perfect blond hair and pink eye mask, I wonder about what's ahead for me. I also wonder at what my friend, the eternal realist, will say about my blazing sex-capade a few hours ago. I'm pretty sure that she'll approve. I return to sleep with a smile on my face.

The bed is empty when I next open my eyes. When I join my friends in the kitchen, I find that they're busy discussing chicken coops, preschool, and hormones—the topics that 40 year-old women tend to discuss. Nobody mentions Jake or asks about what happened, so I'm suspicious of the group, thinking that they've have already discussed it and come to a mutual conclusion. Finally, Jenny looks at me and mentions the unopened condom: "Well, I guess you didn't follow through last night," she says. We all share a laugh about this, and I gleefully fill them in on all the details and my feelings, sharing how I've never felt that luminous before. I am positively glowing. Jenny and Emma give each other a look of giddiness tinged with concern.

Since I can't ski, during the day I slip easily into the role of chauffeur for those who are tackling the slopes. With that job fulfilled, I opt to head to the bar early and hold down a prime table, which tends to coincide with drinking during daylight hours. I can't help but think of Jake all through the day. I find myself having thoughts and cravings I forgot existed. I'm counting the moments until I get to touch him again.

As the skiing day winds down, I pick the girls up as they make their way down from a mid-mountain haunt, Cloud Nine. The girls debrief me on the ski day as we head to The Sky Bar, which is one of the craziest après-ski places in Colorado. It is common to find people dancing on tables and huge booths filled to the brim with happy drinkers. We have a prime spot near the DJ and are surrounded by a bevy of new dance partners. My heart skips as Emma motions to me that she sees Jake arriving. I glance over making eye contact, but we largely keep our distance from one another, respectfully spending time with our own groups. As the girls dance around our table, I feel someone behind me and without turning around, I grab his hand. Sensing his presence, I know it's Jake. I turn to him, our bodies now closely pressing against each other. He leads me out of the party.

In the hallway, we manage to squeeze in a few private moments with a few kisses here and there. There is electricity between us. It is difficult for me to hold back my flustered smile as I stare into his blue eyes. There isn't a lot being said between us, but there isn't a lot that needs to be said. I feel myself wanting, yearning for him again. Our moment together is brief. He tells me of his plan to head to a private party, but he suggests that we meet up later, an offer which I can only smile about.

Back inside the lounge, our table is one of the last to leave, and somehow, we've picked up a trio of Brazilian boys: a freelance journalist, a chef, and another guy who I affectionately name SOB since he claims to be the son of a billionaire. As the bar is closing, they let us know they are staying in Snowmass and need a place to shower before a night out in Aspen. Emma and Jenny are both well into their cocktails at this point and gladly offer up our house for them to clean their bodies. We all hop into a high mountain taxi outside, but it's full; the Brazilians do their best to glom on by standing on the bumper and hitching a ride. The girls have their windows down, shouting and cheering them on. The snow is falling furiously; good sense prevails, and they hop off the car. We carry on with the evening and don't think any more of them until, back at the house, we get a knock on the door. It appears the Brazilians walked here, having nabbed the address from Emma earlier. Now *that* is persistence.

Wine bottles are opened, and the chef rustles around in Emma's fridge, throwing together a surprisingly tasty concoction for us all to munch on. The music is loud, and the house is lively. As the night moves on, conversations deepen and SOB tries to pair off with me. I'm moderately enjoying his attention, noting that he upholds the stereotype of the Latin man who has a way with women. I'm flattered as he keeps gazing into my eyes and telling me how beautiful I am, but I've got Jake on the brain. SOB reaches out for a kiss, but I'm noncommittal, and when a text from Jake arrives—"I'm out with friends at a place called Gray Lady, will you come meet us?"—I can barely call a taxi fast enough. It's snowing out, and I'm in such a hurry to be in the company of this beautiful man once again that I throw on some shoes, grab the first coat I can get my hands on, and forget about any kind of scarf or hat.

As I run out to hop in the taxi, SOB comes chasing after me, saying he wants to join me. He claims that all the taxis are full due to the heavy snow. He just wants a ride, and at this point I don't give a shit, I want to get back with Jake as quickly as possible, so I relent. On the ride to town, he continues to profess his affections for me while also grilling me about where I'm going, and whether Jake is my boyfriend. I say no, but I tell him in the bluntest possible way that I'm leaving as soon as we arrive at Gray Lady. We round the corner of Mill Street and stop just outside the bar. SOB is planting kisses on me, and as the mini-van's door slides open, I see Jake standing outside, waiting for me.

Clearly, I'm a walking, talking hypocrite, because I'm telling myself that I'm serious about this potential relationship with Jake, and that I see a commitment, but in the same breath I'm trading kisses with a young, beautiful Brazilian. I'm not taking it seriously with Jake, despite my intuition that this is real. I have to ask myself: if I wanted him, would

I put myself in such a situation? I decide to focus on Jake and blame my error in judgment it on the air in Aspen.

I speak none of this to Jake, as we head inside to meet his friends. When he offers me a drink, I decline, because we both know that we're not going to be there long. Our hands intertwine as he smiles, reading my mind. We walk back to The Sky Hotel where he is staying. It's pouring snow by now, and I'm completely unprepared in terms of warm headwear. Thankfully, Jake has a Russian-style rabbit fur hat. We stop in silence as he gently places the hat on my head and slowly caresses my face, ensuring that my cold ears are entirely covered.

We walk through the snow together, holding gloved hands, periodically stopping to kiss in the heavy snowfall. It's an incredibly romantic moment, and everything feels so perfect to me. The town is quiet, and the thick snow provides a cloaked feeling of intimacy. When we arrive at his hotel room, there's no hesitation. We're both crystal clear on what's going to happen, and truthfully, I've never wanted someone inside me as much as I want Jake right now. He possesses a softness of touch which, coupled with his sense of control, makes me feel safe but incredibly aroused by his every touch.

We stand face-to-face in the middle of the hotel room. He looks me in the eye and begins describing what he wants to do to me. He delivers this in a way that is tantalizing and dominant, with an element of softness, as though he is seeking my approval. He has the ability to lead my fantasy with his erotic suggestions, but gives me just enough space to explore my desires. A mistake anxious men often make is claiming they want to please the woman, stating something like, "We aren't leaving this bed until you come three times," thereby putting pressure on the situation and giving false expectations.

Most men claim to be out to please the woman, but in actuality the pleasure or reward will be to their ego if they succeed in making a beautiful woman orgasm. It is transparent, and the result is the woman feels like a trophy or prize. Jake does nothing of the sort, but is confident and content with whatever unfolds. He has a plan, but he takes his time, patiently reading my body and my every need.

I pause and wonder if his confidence comes from years of experience. His divorce was finalized eight years ago, and I recoil a bit while contemplating how many women have experienced this pleasure as well. I decide that I don't care: it is my turn. Our bodies are naked. The excitement of feeling and touching this new territory consumes me. After my hands have inspected every inch of his arms and his chest, I gain the confidence to let them slide down, grab him and signal how much I want him.

I'm greeted with an astonishing surprise that I can hardly believe is real. I want to turn on the lights to see if what I'm feeling is actually the extraordinarily generous size my hands surmise. I hold my breath as I become startled by the thought of what I expect this to feel like. I now understand where his masculine confidence stems from. I sense he has experienced this reaction before. He slows things down, gently caressing my hair, looking me in the eye as he slowly enters my body. He takes my breath away as I feel an indescribably fullness of pleasure and pain. I've never felt anything like this before. My heart pounds as I surrender to everything that he has to offer. As our bodies pulse toward climax, he owns me in a way that nobody has owned me before.

I spend the night in his room, dozing and waking several times to repeat our sexual adventures. I wonder if he is actually 50 or 19. The next morning, I feel euphoric and gratified as we say our goodbyes. In the taxi back to Emma's, my mind begins filling with the questions, doubts, and anxieties that most women feel around the concept of sex with a new partner: *should I do that, or not? Will it reflect poorly on me if I sleep with someone so soon after meeting them? Will my friends judge me? Do I regret doing what I did?* All too often, women are judged for our sexual choices. We judge ourselves, we are judged by other women, and we are judged by men. I wonder if Jake will judge me. Did I just fuck up our long-term potential, as Emma's husband Marc had suggested?

Rather than dwelling on these questions, as I've certainly done in the past year, I quickly focus on a few key statements. Namely: I'm a grown-ass woman. If I decide that I want to have sex with somebody, I'm going to have sex. With Jake, I'd have regretted *not* having sex with him.

Smiling to myself, I feel liberated and empowered to have come to these conclusions. By taking my choice back from the usual bullshit doubts around sex, I feel content and fulfilled. I'd wager that Jake feels much the same, too. It was a beautiful experience, and one to be savored, rather than to be internally debated and churned over endlessly. Our connection was clear and rare. I'm glad I took it.

After departing Aspen, I am pleased that Jake and I continue texting. Our connection only grows despite the distance between us. The following week, I was unexpectedly scheduled for knee surgery. I feared my time off would break our bond. Much to my delight, Jake booked a last-minute ticket from New York and rushed to Austin to be by my side. I want to be free from distractions and recover in peace, so I book a hotel room for a staycation of sorts. His flight is delayed, and I'm asleep when he finally arrives at 2:00 am. As he enters the dark hotel room he drops his bag, kneeling on one knee and softly kissing me on my stomach and forehead. I'm ecstatic to be with him again. It's a cold, rainy weekend, so we spend almost the entire time in bed—though, to be honest, we probably would do the same even if the weather were beautiful. An injured knee does not hold us back. We pick up right where we left off, touching constantly, exploring each other's bodies extensively.

Our time together is more than I expected. My fondness for him grows rapidly. I dare say that it is the closest thing to feeling love again since my failed marriage. Recovering from my surgery has me groggy, and drifting in and out of sleep as he watches over me. He takes this quiet moment as an opportunity to check in with his daughter over a phone conversation.

"Emily, I understand how you feel," he says. "I miss you, too, and would be there every minute if I could. I'm proud of you for keeping on track with your science project. I can't wait to see you Saturday and finish it together." He hangs up the phone and sits in silence, watching the rain outside. Alone in the peaceful room, I can feel Jake's intensity and his secure bond with his daughter. I dream that I too can have that same compassionate bond with Jake.

After that weekend in bed, we continued to meet in different cities whenever we could. There was a period where it completely worked. Life just flowed, and we were both so happy about it. As time went on, logistics and life commitments became more challenging. I had Jake pegged as long-term potential, but I was so caught up in our connection that I wasn't giving enough thought to the fact that he lives in New York. As a single parent, I empathized with prioritizing his daughter, but I underestimated the challenge in balancing time, distance ,and our respective children. His tenderness and dedication to his daughter tugs at his heart, and he became isolated in his struggle.

The isolation and shift in behavior evoked an anxious longing in me to know where we were going. I grasped for some sort of guarantee that things would work for us. It increased to the point where I triggered a classic 'DTR' moment, where I asked him to define the relationship. I called him at work, putting him on the spot, pressuring him to tell me where we stand. After a deep conversation, Jake said he'd call me back later that day after thinking about it. When his call came, it wasn't the news I had hoped for: he couldn't commit to our relationship because of his work, and whenever he wasn't working, he needed to be with his daughter. I was taken back to the moment of our first kiss when we knew we wanted to be together, but we didn't know how or what that meant.

In one phone call it was over. He was willing to let it all go.

His decision devastated me. I couldn't understand how it had gone so well for so long, and then all of a sudden, my query had made him realize that it wasn't working for his schedule or his priorities. The one man that I thought was so perfectly available turned out to be the most unavailable. I cried for days, struggling to ground myself by remembering all the great things I have in my life without him. I don't know whether I cried this much over my divorce. It was a tough lesson to learn. I came to fully understand the Legend of Aspen my friends warned me about.

Six

THE COMPLICATIONS

"That fear of missing out on things makes you miss everything."

ETTY HILLESUM

Weeks after I made the fatal DTR move and said a painful goodbye to Jake, I was reading an article on *BuzzFeed* that perfectly described what I'd been through with him. The writer had dubbed it the 'millennial fade,' a situation in modern dating that's primarily reserved for that generation. It occurs after you begin dating and hanging out, and things start moving so quickly that the other party decides to pump the brakes to put some distance between the two of you.

Excuses start filling the vacuum: work takes precedence and the other party suddenly can't find time to meet with you. Thus, the "fade," which is highly painful as it can leave a host of unanswered questions. Another factor contributing to the painful world of modern dating is that everyone has a device in their pockets that allows us to stay in touch at all times, so the specter of that person lingers for months after the moments together have faded.

This unexpected lingering took me by surprise, as I first dated in an era when if you said goodbye, you meant it. You cut the cord and mutually walked away. That's how I'd handled break-ups prior to today's technology, so it was quite an adjustment to find myself in a situation where text messages can ping into my world at all hours and where social media stalking is a hard-to-avoid compulsion. I was guilty of both filthy habits, as was Jake. Some nights I'd be in bed, about to fall asleep, when a message from him would enter my room, jarring my routine and throwing me into another emotional spin cycle. *Why is he texting me? Is he still interested? Are we friends? Or something more than that? Is he just looking for some entertainment?*

It's frustrating, because I had explained to him that I wanted to make a clean cut. Jake is a person that I can't be just friends with; the sexual desire and longing for something bigger is too great. Yet here he is, randomly messaging me on a Tuesday night like an excitable teenager. His presence is a painful reminder of how things ended between us, and the fact that he can't seem to make that disconnect means that the lines of communication are blurred. While he's certainly not a millennial in age—he's 50, for Christ's sake—his lifestyle as a single man in Manhattan is closely aligned with that kind of mentality, where the dating game is seen as an all-you-can-eat buffet, and the next opportunity is never far away. I do my best to move on and put this behind me.

I try to find comfort in my daily routine and ground

myself. I'm relaxing with my kids on a Saturday night when I receive an unexpected text from Alex, who I hadn't heard from in several weeks. I'm midway through eating a bagel smothered in cream cheese, a comfort snack that has replaced the depressing ice cream eating scene. I prod at my phone to reveal a photo of Alex with his shirt off, at his posh athletic club in London. My eyes bulge hungrily. He looks *yummy.*

"Salut babe," he writes. "I am coming to New York for a Sotheby's auction and some other business. I'll be staying at the Mark. Will you come visit me?"

I'm all in.

"Absolutely," I reply, thinking that some time with another man is just what I need to take my mind off of Jake. I convince myself that distraction is the perfect strategy. Energized by my decision, I throw down my bagel and head directly to the gym. As I was slathering on the cream cheese, I was thinking to myself that nobody would be seeing me naked for quite a while. Happily, it seems, I was wrong. I had last seen Alex when he visited Austin around the New Year. Our relationship was vague: were we friends or something more?

While in Austin, he booked a room at the Hotel Saint Ceclia. We met for a drink nearby at Perla's, a charming oyster bar on South Congress. Alex dove into stories of his New Year in Brazil and how he'd been in a remote region, spending time with a shaman who advised him not to have sex, eat spicy food or drink alcohol for 120 days. I was shocked to hear this.

"Why in the hell did you come to Texas?" I replied. "That's pretty much all we do here!"

However, I found that once you take the options of sex

and alcohol off the table, you get to know somebody. During that weekend, we became much closer as friends and bonded greatly in the knowledge that those two obvious activities were off-limits. I was able to get to know him on a much more intimate, detailed level. It helped, too, that by the end of the weekend, his hands were all over me, and he was telling me, "I can't wait until this shaman shit's over. I want to be with you." Hence my excitement this time around. I cherished the opportunity to increase our intimacy and see where things might lead.

In the days ahead of my flight, Jake and I picked up our usual confusing and sporadic connection via texting. The lack of seeing and connecting with Jake frustrated me. I couldn't stop myself from sending a passive "fuck you," so I told him that I'd be in New York that week, but that I wouldn't have time to see him. I wanted him to know that I could be in the same city and resist seeing him. Part of me also wanted to prove to myself that I was in control and could resist him. This was a mistake on my part, as it triggered a few days of back-and-forth texting, both of us vague in our desires. My yearning to see him grew to an unmanageable level. Eventually, we both cave almost simultaneously.

He texts me, "Where are you? I've been trying to reach you. I need to see you when you are in New York."

I decide in the heat of the moment that I will ditch whatever plans I have with Alex to be with Jake.

My valiant effort to numb myself through distraction and passive aggression have created an enormous mess. By this point, I'm sick to my stomach. What had started as a fun-loving trip to see Alex now involves the last man to break my heart. I still genuinely want to work it out with Jake, so I'm thinking that it might be the last chance for us to determine whether there's the possibility of a shared future. But since it's all happening the night before I'm committed to see another man, this conversation couldn't come at a worse time.

I arrive at the Austin airport the next morning, ahead of my 8:00 am flight. I know I need to back out of my date with Alex. I decide honesty is the best policy, so I call Alex and tell him that I can't see him, as I've become involved in a situation with another man. It's messing with my head in a major way.

He doesn't understand. His response is forceful. "Babe, get on the plane and stick to the plan and meet me at the Mark. Once we are together, everything will be fine." When I protest, he takes things up a notch or seven. "I travel all over the world and I meet all kinds of people," he says. "I understand that we've been back and forth on friendship, but I had some things to sort through with my divorce. I'm at the point now where I want to be with someone, and I want to see where this goes. I want to be in a relationship."

These words blow my mind, as I thought I was heading to New York purely to have our usual casual fun. Now, he's playing the relationship card, and forcing me to choose between him and Jake. The shitty thing is that I'm the one to blame, because I've put myself in this situation. My mind is racing the entire flight there. I try to make sense of this new development with Alex and decide what's best for me. When I arrive, Alex and I meet at the Baccarat Bar on the Upper East Side, a sexy and glamorous hideaway. Of course, he has champagne waiting for me, and he plants a huge kiss on my lips. He's so happy to see me that he's practically glowing.

He asks me to lay out all my cards, and since he's so patient and kind, I do. I tell him that I've gotten myself into a situation where I'm emotionally attached to someone, even after our break-up, and it's been a back-and-forth disturbing roller coaster. I don't know whether or not Jake and I have a future, but what I'm sure of is that I'm not in a healthy or strong enough place to be able to engage with Alex in the way he deserves. I'm looking him in the eye as I say all of this, but he's just not having it. He schools me on the ways of men and chastises Jake's behavior for casting me aside. He tries to dismiss it all as trivial by asking me to move past it. But if it were that easy, I would've done that already.

Alex makes it clear that he's done bouncing around between partners. "Even when we first met, I felt like you were someone I could take from the White House to the doghouse. Kelly, you'd be the perfect mate for me," he says. I'm flattered, but up until this conversation I'd mostly considered him a friend, so I'm having a hard time shifting out of that gear. I'm attracted to him, but do I belong in Alex's world? His is one of sophistication, culture, and art, and it's not one I've ever felt aligns with my identity.

As Alex begins laying out his plans for our evening together—a cocktail reception with Bill Clinton, then dinner with the Beretta family, a party hosted by Valentino's goddaughter, and an after-party in Soho—my mind is swimming. I can't cope, and I tell him so. He still can't believe it and begins a final plea, complete with accusations of leaving him high and dry. I tell him flat out that I'm not coping with this situation. I need to make a beeline for Whitney's safehouse in Soho, where I can regroup and meet with him at a later date, when I'm in a clearer frame of mind.

At last, he relents and, always a gentleman, offers a ride. The first stop is the Adolphus Hotel, where Alex is due to speak at a financial conference for Apollo Global Management. Because I seem to enjoy complicating my life, I'm heading to Cipriani-Grand Central Station to have a friendly cocktail with Timothy, who I've also been texting with ahead of my flight. As we make our way down Park Ave, Alex insists on stopping at a Coffee Bean & Tea Leaf store to get his almond milk cappuccino. While Alex orders his coffee, all I can think about is how segmented my life has become and how problematic I've made things for myself. Did I need to see all three of them in one trip? I'm on the verge of a panic attack when I realize that, even though I've gone to such great lengths to keep my life compartmentalized, the worlds of all three of the men in my life could potentially overlap at this Coffee Bean and Tea Leaf on the 400 block of Park Avenue.

I don't live in this city, but every time I've visited lately, its sectors have been neatly divided for me. Timothy (New York) lives on the Upper West Side, and never goes past 45th Street after 6:00pm unless it's for a weekend dinner reservation. When Alex (London) comes to town, he only stays in Upper East Side hotels, The Pierre or the Mark, for example. Jake (Aspen) is trendier in his tastes, living in the Flatiron district and rarely venturing north of 45th Street.

The 400 block of Park Avenue is where all of their lives could potentially collide. London has a conference nearby, and both New York's and Aspen's offices are right there, too. It's only while standing in the coffee shop that this realization hits me, that all three might be in the same place at the same time. I am paralyzed with fear. If the three of them met socially and I wasn't there, I'm sure they would all get along fabulously. But with me there, I doubt that. Too many questions and expectations. London would have been unhappy to learn that I was skipping out on our plans to meet up with Aspen, and Aspen didn't think I was seeing anyone else at all—which, *technically*, I wasn't.

I decide that I've got to get out of here ASAP. Alex senses I am flustered and offers to leave the shop. My upper lip is moist with sweat as I tell him I need some fresh air. I hurriedly say goodbye to him and begin walking south to Grand Central Station. Once inside, I take a breath and feel calmed by the crowd flowing in and out. The elegant, four-faced clock tells me that I'm a few minutes early, so I occupy myself with looking up at the sea-green ceiling and astrological rendering. My eyes pause on the two-faced Gemini as I feel a wave of guilt wash over me. I arrive at Cipriani, and Timothy looks great. He kisses me on the cheek, and we pick up exactly where we left off. I always feel good in his presence. It's nice to have someone so smart and powerful in my corner.

I tell him a little about my situation with Jake, and he responds with how wrong it is for me and that I deserve to be treated better. I can't help but realize that was Alex's same perspective on the situation. I suppose men understand men. Timothy shares that he's dating a retired Victoria's Secret model he says is "crazy." Despite myself, I feel envious of this woman, because he uses that word as a result of her decision to speak up about something that she didn't like. I think that I'd like to be called crazy one day for speaking up like that. I'm irked how men call it *crazy* when a woman stands up for her character and principles—traits men attempt to display at all times.

After a relaxing glass of wine and invigorating reminiscing

at Cipriani, I catch an Uber down to Jake's apartment. The ride downtown is long and I find my impatience and anxiety growing. I haven't seen him in a while, and I don't know what to expect. Perhaps my visions of our compatibility are all made up in my head and I'll regret my determination to see him.

I arrive wearing a tight gray knee-length turtleneck dress: sexy, yet sophisticated. Our eyes lock when he opens the door; we simultaneously take a deep breath as I watch his eyes trace my body and take me in. I can't wait to feel his hands on me. We become reacquainted as we discuss plans for dinner, but the conversation quickly becomes whether we should have sex before or afterwards. It's a dumb conversation because we both already know the answer to that: sex first, food later. We never make it out to dinner. Instead, Jake volunteers to pick up some food from an Asian place around the corner. After eating, sex is on the agenda again. While I can't get enough of him touching me, I feel strangely empty after our intimate time together. The time passes quickly; it is already 11:00 pm, and he's asleep. Although he is next to me, I feel alone and disappointed as I look out his window at the Clock Tower of the Met Life building. I wonder if I've done something wrong to push him away. I wonder if I should be here at all.

I gave up an elegant night in Manhattan and all these adventures with Alex just to come here for sex. It wasn't that I felt used, because he wasn't using me. I'd done it to myself by creating so many expectations around this get-together after our back-and-forth texting earlier in the week. I knew I still had feelings for Aspen, but if that was true, would I be feeling so unfulfilled by this "ordinary" night with him?

I wanted more, but I still didn't know if he could give me more. I slowly pad out of the bedroom into the living room. Feeling detached and cold, I lay on his crisp leather couch, wondering why I felt as though I was missing out on something when I had felt so sure this is what I wanted.

On the table, I see our iPhones sitting side-by-side. I can't help myself: I light up his screen. One missed call and a text from "Melissa." I want to throw the fucking phone out the window. I calmly remind myself that she could be anyone; an assistant, perhaps. Jenny's voice pops in my head: "Really, Kelly, an assistant calling at 9:45 pm?" I take a breath, and remember this is dating in Manhattan, and this is the Legend of Aspen in action.

I put his phone down and check my own, where I see that Alex has texted me a photo of himself looking dapper in a tuxedo. "Have you figured out that you made a mistake yet?" he writes.

Still wondering who the hell Melissa is, I respond, "Yeah, I suppose I did." We agree to meet tomorrow. Exhausted, I head back to bed and try to get a good night's sleep beside Jake, but I don't feel comfortable. I long for the connection that we used to have. I'm still distraught how easily he had let me go. Those emotions are barely buried beneath the surface.

The next morning, I wake up in his arms. I breathe in, taking in all of him and bringing our naked bodies closer. I wrap my leg around him and feel him already hard against my stomach. I can't keep my hands off of him, which leads to our usual vigorous round of sex, after which he lovingly brings me coffee in bed. The morning is so perfect. Once again, confusion sets in as I start to second-guess myself.

I'm scheduled to be in NYC for two nights, so over coffee,

we begin discussing our plans for the day. He tells me that he has a dinner tonight, which he'll try to cancel. He says he'll call me from work later to confirm our plans. He kisses me on the forehead and leaves for the office, while I sit waiting for the inevitable small push-away that I always receive after our time together.

Hours later, I receive a call from Jake and brace myself: here it comes. "I loved having you here last night, but I can't get out of my dinner obligation tonight," he says. "I probably won't be home until midnight, which won't give us any time together. So will you be okay on your own tonight?" Before I have a chance to answer, he shuts me down. "I have to run, but let me know the next time you are back in New York," he says. Just like that, I'm discarded once again. I don't know if I should be happy or sad that I knew this was coming and that I already have plans to see Alex. Was I protecting myself or hurting myself?

I am emotionally exhausted, but having anticipated this outcome, I look forward to getting on with my day. My Uber SUV makes its way past Washington Park and turns to make the slow crawl up Park Avenue toward the Mark Hotel. I stare blankly out the window, trying to take comfort in the organized chaos of the city. Still, I feel the tears welling up. My disappointment is overwhelming. My lungs and chest are burning as I swallow and choke back my need to scream out and cry. Why did I want this to work out with Jake? I question if my emptiness is a backlash against our sexual intimacy.

I am learning a hard lesson on why it isn't a good idea to engage in deep sexual intimacy without the grounding of a relationship to back it up. The lack of understanding leads to many hurtful, distorted versions of reality in my head. Perhaps I'm too old? Perhaps I have too many kids? Why didn't he want this the way I wanted it? As I have these thoughts, I realize that I stepped out of his door and into the arms of another man. How could I blame Jake? Whatever he was going through, or whatever was on his mind, my behavior must be a thousand times worse.

I can't sort through my own confusion, much less guess what he is thinking. I want something more. I want to be understood, comforted, and taken care of. I am struck by my immediate thought of Michael. In my deep hurt and pain, I want the comfort of his embrace and the quiet calm he brings to me. I decide to text Michael, and share the honesty of my self-made madness.

"I'm sad," I type. "I think I have officially become a player." Just the mere act of reaching out to him makes me feel better.

"Call me. I just missed a flight to London," he writes.

I'll bet he knows exactly what I'm talking about. When we first started dating, he was skeptical of me coming out of a divorce and being with the first person I came across: him. Back then, he had asked me if I was a player, and I replied honestly that I didn't know what that meant. With a smile, he said, "I think you'll find out. It's going to be inevitable for you." In the midst of my inner turmoil and the attendant chaos, it turns out that Michael was exactly right.

I wonder if his girlfriend is by his side or if things between them have ended. I pick up the phone. My thumb is ready to press the green button to call him, but I know I can't. Part of me wants to blame this mess on Michael. If we were together, I wouldn't be in this world of pain.

As the minutes tick by, Michael texts again. "Where are you?" he asks. "Please call. I can use the entertainment." But

I just can't. I put the phone back in my bag. I take a deep breath, deciding to shift my feelings and look forward to the day I know I will have with Alex, enveloped in the distracting fun that he can provide so well. It's a gorgeous spring day. I admire the cherry blossoms and the spring light that glow throughout the city. As I pull up to the Mark, I feel a sense of adventure and renewed possibility.

Alex has planned another full day of exciting meetings, parties, cocktails, and any other event you could describe. I feel exhausted just listening to his day. My lack of sleep and my emotional distress have left me less than lively, but I follow his lead and attempt to feed off his energy. When would I ever have an opportunity to go to a Sotheby's auction or the Frieze Art Fair with such a master of this kingdom? At the Frieze, Alex has a meeting scheduled with an art museum in London that is soliciting a donation for an addition to its building. Although he is eclectic and vivacious, adding his name to a building is too passé and not his style. He has other things in mind.

His brilliant idea is to commission an art piece for the museum that would draw extra revenue and attendance to the museum. The idea? A solid gold toilet seat. I am speechless. He is certainly out-there in his thinking, way beyond mine. However, he does have a point. I listen intently as he describes his plan and the flock of people that would come to take selfies on the toilet. I must hand it to him: Alex knows how to take it to another level.

My mind drifts and the conversations of the crowd fade in the background. Is this what I want for my life? Could I keep up with Alex and his pace, or would his expectations for aesthetic perfection consume me? Would I be the already perfect Bach chair that he modifies with a singed branding? Again, my exhaustion and rocky emotions take me in another direction. I am overwhelmed with a wave of sadness as I realize Alex and I simply cannot and will not be together either. Although I have known this all along, he is now no longer a fun party partner. He represents just another face of my unquenchable thirst for deep love, which constantly leads me astray.

Alex and I conclude our long day and head back to his room at the Mark, which is sometimes described as New York's most boldly lavish hotel. Humorously, those adjectives form the perfect description for Alex, too. His busy day flows into the night with plans involving more time with the fabulous art crowd, but my enthusiasm has truly waned.

He senses that I am tired, even while he is running hard. We agree that the best thing is for us to separate before he starts his evening. I am somewhat relieved to leave him. I need to rest. It is 7:00 pm in Manhattan, and I have no idea where I am going to go or what will happen next. Every moment of the last 72 hours has been unpredictable and painful, yet so awakening. I sit on the sofa of Alex's ostentatious suite and wonder where I will go next. I hear him start the shower. He calls out, "Babe, would you mind calling down to see if my suit is back from being pressed? Also, check on my latte? It should be here by now."

I take pleasure in handling these small tasks for him, but Alex continues mumbling something to me in the shower, and I decide that the distance and distraction of his shower provides the best time for me to depart.

"Alex, love, I am leaving now," I call out over the muffled sounds of the shower.

"What? Now? Not yet, babe—please wait," he protests. I lie and tell him Whitney is waiting for me. In reality, I have found myself homeless in Manhattan and want to run from this city as fast as I can. Alex says he understands. As I make my way to the door he pops his head out of the shower and looks at me in a deep and knowing way. "The Chateau in August?" he asks. I nod. "Yes, the Chateau in August."

I ride down the elevator wondering where I'll go. I know I could call Timothy. He would take me in and take care of me in a second. He's just around the corner, and even if he isn't there, his doorman will ensure my comfort. I dismiss the idea. I've already caused myself enough trouble. My every turn towards men has taught me that it is time to turn toward myself. I want out of the city, and I want out now. Manhattan has taken me in, awakened my soul and even become my second home. Now, she has shown me the dark consequences of my deepest fears.

The consequences of my fear have left me alone and confused. Fear of missing out is something that grips all of us at one time or another, but what was it I was really afraid of? Being in one place while dreaming of another is a dangerous thing to do. But I felt there was more to it. It wasn't that I was merely afraid of missing an extravagant evening in Manhattan for a loving evening at home. FOMO was a symptom of what I needed to understand. What prompted my FOMO and the distracting thought of Alex that robbed me of my genuine moment with Jake? I admitted to myself that I was afraid of loving without a guarantee. I was afraid of telling Jake that I am worthy and I deserve more. I was afraid of showing weakness.

It is too late to catch a flight out, but in my desire to flee,

I head to JFK and get as close to the exit as I can. I take solace in the quiet and slow pace of the traffic on the way out to the airport. I reflect on my time with Alex and feel a sense of closure and an understanding of what he brought to my life. I remind myself that I never had expectations that it would be any more than exactly what it was. Alex and I are like kindred wild horses, running side by side, giving one another the occasional nuzzle. We have an unspoken appreciation for where the other is in life and what the other was searching for. Our pace for life is on point and perhaps unmatched by any other partner. Our mutual desire to live life in a curious, nomadic, and unconventional way is understood and never judged by the other. He reminds me of my unbridled spirit and to live my life the way I want to live it.

As my Uber arrives at the shittiest of shitty hotels outside of JFK, I switch my phone to airplane mode to shut down the world outside. After checking in, I quickly turn on the shower, sit down, and cry for what seems like hours. I had tricked myself into thinking so many things were true. Yet each time, reality won out, devastating me. Why couldn't I just pick one of my options and stick with it? Why was I constantly searching for someone, and why couldn't I find what I was looking for?

The next morning, I switch off airplane mode ahead of my 5:30 am flight. I am greeted by a voicemail from Jake. He says how great it was to see me. He loved sharing time together and the simplicity of taking care of me and bringing me food for a cozy night in. I fall deep into the warmth of his voice. I want to believe in him. I want to take a risk. Is Jake genuine, or is Jake just an ass who kicked me out of Manhattan?

At the time, I was comparing every aspect of the

experience against what I was missing out on with Alex, so of course a quiet night in Manhattan was going to disappoint. Add to that the anxiety of getting caught jumping between men, and it was all too overwhelming and nutty.

All I can think about is my true desire to rebuild my family and how much I want to be with my children. I want to have them as close to me as possible: a sleepover in my bed with my girls, to be grounded in the reality of what I really do have. I question if whatever I was chasing in New York genuinely existed—unlike my family, which absolutely does.

Seven

GIRL TIME

"Sex appeal is fifty percent what you've got and fifty percent what people think you've got."

SOPHIA LOREN

After the chaos of Manhattan, I've decided to take a break from men. I'm excited for my upcoming spring vacation to the British Virgin Islands. Time on the beach, sunny islands and rum—just what the doctor ordered. I'm running late and have a full travel day ahead of me. I have to make a connection in Miami, get a taxi in Saint John's, and take a ferry to Tortola. It is a tight schedule, to say the least.

As I'm racing to the airport, I receive a call from the preschool telling me I need to come speak with the teacher. It seems my three-year-old son, Jagger, has adopted a new word in his vocabulary. It starts with 'F' and ends with 'uck.' When I hear the news and end the call, I say that word aloud several times. 'Fuck' is exactly right. I don't need this today, not at all. I'm ready for my break and looking forward to getting out of town. I pound my palm on the steering wheel. I can either face the music or keep my plans. In a snap, I turn the car around, speed down the freeway and head back to school.

As I drive, I start to feel the stress of rescheduling my travel. That anxiety quickly shifts to my children and to my parenting skills. I can't help but feel that I am failing in a major way. How could this happen? My baby, my three-year-old, cursing like a sailor already? None of the older children did this. This behavior was unheard of when I was married. I take on a tremendous amount of self-blame and guilt. *Did I say 'fuck' in front of him?* I'm 100 percent sure that I have. *How often? In what context? How am I going to reverse this?* I worry it's a slippery slope that will land him kicked out of preschool! How am I going to possibly raise four children as a single mother? They deserve the best life possible, and I feel as though I am already failing.

Turning into the school parking lot, my heart is heavy and my pulse is racing. I round the corner to see multiple fire trucks parked in front. I'm immediately concerned about an emergency, but then recall that it's fireman day. The tiny children begin filing out the door to greet the firemen and inspect the shiny trucks. While the children are outside, I meet with the school director and Jagger's teacher. After a thorough discussion about my son's behavior and emotional balance, I'm determined that he will survive this incident. I'm not sure that his preschool spot is secure, but for now we will live another day. I'm able to successfully convince the teacher that he likely misspoke by blending 'fire' and 'truck.' I think they buy it, but they probably have a laugh amongst themselves as soon as we leave. Jagger is dismissed for the day.

Jagger and I walk hand-in-hand down the narrow, tiled hallway in silence, carrying glitter-coated artworks, a full backpack and an empty Spider-Man lunchbox. As we reach the car, I lift his miniature body up to place him in the car seat. Standing in the empty parking lot, I pause for a long hug, before he finally says, "Mommy, I love you so, so, so, so much." The combination of stress, relief, and affection is enough to bring me to tears. I realize Jagger has given me a gift by forcing me to take a short pause from my frantic running. Meanwhile, I've missed my flight. *Fuck* indeed, son!

I was invited to the British Virgin Islands—known affectionately by locals as the BVIS—by a good friend, Thomas Bailey. He is a British real estate developer who has a lovely estate house on a hillside, equipped with several private bungalows. Bailey is a warm, carefree man in his 50s who's happy to play host to his long list of intriguing friends. He's single, without children, and dates models almost exclusively, but when you're a wealthy man in the BVIS, I guess that's the lifestyle that works best. Although I'm here by myself this time, Bailey is so welcoming that I make a mental note to ask whether I can bring my kids back another time.

Bailey's other visitors this weekend include couples from the UK and Spain, as well as a girl in town from Brazil and several local friends. Most of my experience with beach towns has entailed visiting a single island, but the BVIS are all about boating, sailing, and island-hopping. One of its main cities, Tortola, is a financial hub where a lot of attorneys are based, working on offshore mergers, acquisitions, and tracking embezzlements such as Bernie Madoff's. The significant money attached to these deals brings in a lot of business brains from throughout the world, as well as more than a few sharks who are forever circling and angling for their chance at long-term wealth. Bailey is heavily involved in this world, and I'm intrigued at the thought of meeting his friends.

In time, I begin gravitating toward a specific group of Baily's friends, intelligent women who live on the island when they're not traveling to London or Moscow for business. One woman in particular, makes a big impression on me. Her name is Julie. She's 32, beautiful with long fire red hair, and very aggressive in her personality. She's the complete opposite of me, in that she's bold and vivacious.

Since the Manhattan chaos, my mind has been firmly fixed on avoiding men. This trip, I'm not even looking at a single male. Of course I haven't dropped my bad habit of texting Jake, but other than that they're off my radar. I'm taking a man break, completely uninterested. This mindset leads me to spend more time with Julie than I usually might, and I find myself being pulled to her like iron filings to a magnet. As she guides me out of my comfort zone, she's also creating some sexual tension, which isn't apparent to me. Throughout the weekend, we're regularly partnered together during our group activities, to the point where I become somewhat reliant on her, and I sense that she enjoys playing that role. It's not a particularly deep emotional connection, but it's the type of bond that I've found throughout my life when in the company of a man who is assertive and confident.

I feel all of that with Julie, and it's blowing my mind a little, throwing up all sorts of questions. On my last day in the BVIs, there's a racing event called The Poker Run. The event attracts boats of all kinds that hop from island to island, picking up a card at each stop. The objective is to assemble a strong poker hand, and at the final port, the best hand wins the race. We leisurely trail the race spending some time on each island, drinking cocktails, swimming, and making new friends.

The Poker Run starts early in the morning, and about halfway through the race, we stop at Cooper Island for lunch at the Beach Club. We spot a table that has assembled an impromptu band, including a guitar and a banjo. Naturally, Julie can't resist and joins them, playing spoons and encouraging me to dance.

I'm having a fantastic time, not thinking about men whatsoever in this completely different world where I've had little connection to reality. Naturally enough for this isolated part of the world, there's little cell phone coverage, and in such an engaging social environment, there seems little need to connect with the outside world. During a moment of downtime, my phone connects to wi-fi and pings with text messages. I receive one from Jake: it's a photo of he and his daughter on a trip together. My heart aches as I'm reminded what a caring and dedicated father he is. God, I miss him, but part of my objective for the trip is to let that go.

A second text arrives. "Are you on vacation?" asks Michael. He must have seen a photo I posted to social media. "Who are you with?" He's taking a familiar, curious tone, which can sometimes feel judgmental. It certainly does in this moment, when I'm a few rums deep into my day of socializing. I'm uninterested in having a conversation, so I ignore him.

The last time I'd spoken to Michael, prior to my Manhattan texts, he told me that he was struggling with his girlfriend. Apparently she always wants to listen to loud dubstep music at night, which hurts his ears. I had to laugh. My response to both of these complaints was the same: she's 25, you're 50. He said he loved her, but questioned the hardship of the age gap, and it was taking its toll on the relationship. This triggered a glimmer of possibility at the back of my mind that maybe, just maybe, he'd come back from Europe after the summer, and we'd have another chance at becoming close again.

The day continues with sailing and drinking. Julie grabs life by the balls. I'm envious of her sense of recklessness. I watch her as she effortlessly climbs to the top of the boat's bridge. She has a bottle of Veuve Clicquot and strikes Leonardo DiCaprio's famous *"I'm the king of the world!"* pose. She drinks champagne from the bottle as the wind whisks through her hair. She is alive, bold, and magnetic. I stand timidly on the deck below for quite a while, admiring her and her life.

Julie looks down and encourages me to climb up and shake my ass. I respond with a quiet, "I don't think I can do that." I know I am not a table-dancing kind of girl, but I admire those who are, as it requires an element of "I don't give a fuck" that I would like to have myself. She sends down another coaxing comment. "C'mon, Kelly, your ass is too perfect not to be up here bouncing in the wind." I do like her flattery.

"Come on, I will take care of you up here," she says. "You are safe with me." I very seriously doubt that I will be safe, but I decide to take the chance anyway. I make the unsafe and unapproved route up the slippery front. If this were sanctioned, I tell myself, there would be a ladder. I reach the top and look down at the waves rushing past the boat. The height of the bridge emphasizes the motion of the waves, imparting a gentle rocking, soothing feeling as I relax and feel the wind in my face.

Julie is laughing at me. She knows I'm terrified, and she is pleased with herself for pushing me into a risky situation. She passes me the champagne bottle. My grip is so tight that I don't want to make another unsafe move. I'm paralyzed with fear. She knows it, and laughs as she pours the champagne in my mouth. I relax a bit, soothed by a false sense of security.

I know I'm not safe and that I could fall at any minute, but I stop worrying and relish the adrenalin. I take in the wind, the sun, and the ocean as we cruise past Devil's Bay. I, too, am alive and free. I can't stay in the moment for very long, however, as my anxiety takes hold, and I think of other reasons to dismount. High-speed yachts and eyelash extensions, I learn, do not mix: I've probably lost $40 in lashes in the last five minutes. Time to get down!

After a long day of sailing we arrive at Richard Branson's Mosquito Island and drop anchor. Michael is annoyingly still on my mind, and we are close enough to an island to receive a signal again. Another text from Michael pings in. It's much longer, seemingly in response to my silence.

"I want to send you something, and it's from the most sincere place in my heart," he writes. "I understand all the troubles and the turmoil that you're going through. You're struggling trying to find your way. I'm just struggling, trying to find my way, as well. I hope we both get sorted soon."

My first thought is that he's going to jump off a bridge. I've never read anything like that from him, or from anyone in my life. I could feel the despair oozing from every word. It left me feeling sad and confused, despite my beautiful surroundings.

Again I lose the signal, until we drift slightly closer to the

the final port of The Poker Run, Virgin Gorda. It is about 7:00 pm. Michael is in Europe, so that's closer to 1:00 am for him. I'm walking around, holding my cell phone high in the air and praying to the wi-fi gods that I find a connection; anything that'll let me find out what's going on with him. Finally, I'm able to send a message asking him whether everything is okay. The next thing that appears on my screen is a grainy picture of the backside of a bride and groom. He's kissing her. The groom's hands are wrapped around her youthful, thin waist. All I can see is the back of her bridal hair laced in flowers, and the wedding band on the groom's hand.

Holy shit, did he just get married?!

I feel like somebody just hit me in the face with a frying pan. I furiously tap out a quick response. "I guess we're sorted, then," I write. He responds, "Yes. I hope we're sorted." Is Michael literally married? I'm so confused. Was I so hopeful of our reconciliation that I had become blind to his drive for marriage? Was I getting my signals crossed?

Julie is by my side, and she can see how upset I am. We decide not to discuss the story any further than Julie's single comment: "You never can tell what men are actually thinking, especially by a single photo," she says. "I wouldn't over-think it."

We're still in our swimsuits, as the weather is beautiful tonight, and she leads me down to the water, where we slowly wade in. She's gentle and doesn't pry for details, but she knows the basic outline: a man has hurt me. She gives me a hug to comfort me, which soon turns into a kiss, which leads to making out.

It's a surreal experience, to be making out with this beautiful young woman in the water of the Caribbean Islands, beneath the stars and a full moon, yet here I am. I have not anticipated this moment, yet it feels right, because all weekend I've been as drawn to her as I've been to men in the past. I soon learn that there's something about the way a woman kisses that's very soft and tender, yet sexual at the same time. Distraught as I was by Michael's photo, I feel cared-for and caressed by Julie, who has somehow timed it so well that she gives me exactly what I need.

It doesn't go much further. We come out of the water, and Bailey can see that I'm upset by something, so he kindly puts us on a ferry and takes us home. Up until that time with Julie, I'd never kissed a girl, but I'm sure a lot of women have experienced a similar kind of moment with the same sex. It's only when you're in that situation that you get a true feeling for whether or not it's right for you. Kissing Julie was so short that I don't quite have a definitive answer either way, but I was still glad that she took the initiative to give me a taste of it. I couldn't have asked for a kinder, gentler first kiss.

That night gave me a greater understanding of the transient nature of human attraction. If there's a connection, then it makes sense to seize that moment and see where it leads. Whether it's with the opposite gender or the same, it doesn't matter. The heart wants what it wants. I feel as though social norms often mean that quite a few people deny or refuse their true attractions because they're unsure of how it might be perceived by those around them. Even though my moment with Julie was abrupt, it was still preceded by a built-up sexual attraction. In the past, I'd been attracted to 6'5" men with wavy, dark hair, yet both my attraction to Michael—a 5'11" bald man—and Julie show that to try to put labels on such an intangible concept is foolhardy and short-sighted. I'd certainly been guilty of thinking that I have a 'type,' but those kisses in the water opened my eyes to the truth of the matter.

My time with Julie was nothing more than a beautiful Caribbean friendship, and it went to the next level after a long day of drinking, sailing, and a dash of heartache. Our goodbye was genuine, as we weren't planning to see each other again. With a man, the usual protocol is to exchange numbers and keep in touch. But she lives on an island, and I live in Texas.

I don't think she's even that into women. It was just a nice gesture of comfort in a time of need, just as I'd experienced with men in my past. Our goodbye wasn't awkward, and neither of us rushed to keep it hush-hush. Instead, we both seemed to accept that it happened, it felt right at the time, and we were mutually happy to continue with our lives as before.

Eight

WHAT A YEAR

"For last year's words belong to last year's language and next year's words await another voice."

T.S. ELIOT

When I arrive home from the BVIs on Sunday night, the kids are asleep. Kerry, my live-in manny—male nanny—is there to greet me. He's a fun-loving, red-headed guy from the Northeast who the kids adore playing with. He relates well to the boys with the the kind of physical play that men can provide. I've found him to be an excellent way to balance a single-mother household.

Once I drop my bags and get settled, Kerry and I sit down to chat about the week and events to come. Each Sunday, I prepare a schedule: pick-ups, drop-offs, play dates, areas for improvement, homework, meal planning. There's a lot to cover, yet I sense Kerry's attention drifting back to *Silicon Valley* on HBO, so I decide to summarize later via email and let him enjoy the rest of his night. I quickly check in on my electronic life, reviewing email and social media for the week. There is nothing about Michael's wedding on Facebook. Surely someone would have mentioned the celebration. I can't help but wonder if he is actually married or if the text and photo had another intention that was lost on me.

As I drag myself to my room, bone-tired, I think about the day ahead and how mothers are expected to be like superheroes who can adapt to any situation while being able to answer any question the kids might ask, such as "What is heaven?" or "Where do babies come from?" A lot of the pressure, admittedly, is self-imposed: as a mother, I want to be the best, so I put high demands on myself to know and understand nutrition, health, education, sports, friends, and external influences, as well as being a professional driver, among many other roles. The list of areas of expertise is long and exhaustive.

How, exactly, did I wind up with such responsibility? I still can't quite fathom that this is my life. It feels heavy, and I know that I need to slow down. Craving some me-time, I take a warm bath then crawl into bed at 8:37 pm.

As the spring turns to summer, I find myself taking what would be a final trip in my year of dating dangerously. At Whitney's generous invitation, it's a return to the Hamptons. It's a last-minute day trip that comes about after I tell her that I'm in New York City for work. She invites me to take the train out to see her and review what has been the most exciting, challenging, and fulfilling year of my life. With Whitney, there's never a dull moment, so when I arrive, I'm not surprised to find that she has played matchmaker (as usual) and is hosting an eclectic mix of people. We play games, hang out on the beach and walk around Southampton together.

Taking in the sights of South Hampton, I can't help but feel a tinge of loneliness. I recall my adventures of the last few months and realize how much I've come to learn about things that matter in a relationship. I haven't heard from Michael. However, I can't shake the undeniable soul connection that we have. His ability to truly see me is a treasure I long for. I wonder if I will have to live my life with a lingering feeling of a love that never knew its full potential. I've learned the importance of being patient and comfortable with the unknown. Perhaps in time the nature of our relationship will reveal itself.

I'm unusually quiet and distant. Whitney stops me on our walk to ask if I am ok. I respond that I am, but I'm still so lost in thought. It dawns on me how much the fear of loss has dominated my search for love. Fear has caused me to miss genuine moments, reach for distraction, and chase false securities. I can't help but feel self-preservation has made me overlook something special. What if I took a risk in being exposed and being defenseless even if there were no guarantees? My mind flashes to my time in Aspen when my desire overrode my fear. I remember how exuberant and alive I felt with Jake. Although I never could lock down a guaranteed commitment, I felt proud that my heart remained fearless and always willing to give him a chance.

Later that night, things begin to come full circle for me when we wind up at the Southampton Social Club, the place where I met Timothy almost twelve months earlier. It's much livelier than it was last year, with plenty of people dancing and mingling, yet I feel a sense of inner peace and familiarity. After navigating that year, I know that I can weather any storm. My enhanced self-confidence is brought into sharp focus by a couple of younger single girls that Whitney invited from the city, Kendra and Jamie. Though neither would likely admit it, I can sense their mutual uncertainty and anxiety from across the room. They're both bouncing around between the bar and dance floor, and neither seems to know exactly what they're looking for.

I can relate to this feeling exactly, as I'm sure I gave off the exact same vibe last year. One of them spots a table of exotically handsome guys nearby, but they're both too timid and shy to approach. I look over, acknowledge their rugged sex appeal, and look back at the girls. I know that it's only a matter of time before we're approached, and I caution the girls as such. A few minutes later, Kendra is quick to point out that the handsome guys are surrounded by several girls, long legs and long, blond hair flying everywhere. Two of the guys are making out with their new friends. Kendra expresses her disappointment and wants to move on, thinking we've lost that battle. Again, I dismiss her concerns, and suggest that, with some patience, what will be will be.

Kendra relaxes and takes my advice, and for a while we laugh and watch Whitney as she roams the room, wearing a unicorn's head, causing mayhem and loving life. Sure enough, when I next look over, two of the guys have migrated outside of their bottle-service area to a table just behind us. Kendra and Jamie noticeably tense up, but I'm still filled with a sense of calmness. I'm no longer searching, and I'm happy to relax and see what the night brings us. One of the men finally approach us and appears reluctant to speak, it seems he speaks Spanish and a little broken English. I have neither the patience nor tolerance to engage in this conversation, despite his sheer gorgeousness: olive skin, thick, flowing dark hair, and well-toned arms.

I have no idea what he's saying. Kendra, the peppy brunette in our group, soon sweeps in. It turns out she speaks Spanish, so she slips into the role of translator between the guy I'm talking to and the guy she's talking to, who is introduced as their *entrenador*, or coach. They're polo players in town to play competitively for a few months before moving on to the United Kingdom. Amid the music I gather snippets about the recent Veuve Clicquot Classic that took place in Manhattan a few weeks earlier. The story piques my interest, and we engage in conversation amongst random translations. Our time together is mostly about dancing, drinking cocktails, and smiling at each other. After a full evening of nodding politely, we decide to move on.

Outside of the noisy club environment, our inability to properly communicate with one another is more pronounced. Kendra quietly confides that she's concerned about translating what to do next. I tell her to do nothing and just go with the flow, though if she doesn't like where things are going, she needs to speak up. Something gets lost in translation, and Marcos and the *entrenador* wind up in our taxi on the way home to Whitney's.

Marcos Garcia Del Rio is a young polo player from Argentina who was born into a family of successful athletes. He exudes sexuality that is almost indescribable. His long, thick hair curls from underneath his cap. He has an aura of tradition and respect. At the same time, his tattoos, five o'clock shadow, and rugged collection of necklaces hint at his rebellious and free nature. His hands are strong yet sensitive. I imagine that a man who understands the delicate sensitivities of horses would be very in tune with the sensitivity of a woman's body. He is unfamiliar to me in so many ways, yet I want to know more. I become entranced with his stories of polo and transporting ponies around the world.

We pair off and head to a cozy spot by the pool. We start kissing and cuddling. Through broken English, I come to understand that he has a three-year-old girl and was in a relationship that ended only a few months earlier. I quickly establish that he's a kindhearted person who is based in South America half the year, then spends the rest between the Hamptons and the UK.

"I live on the road, and it's very hard," he tells me. "I'm trying to find the right person to fit into my life."

I feel a real empathy for Marcos, as it's a tender, honest exchange with a stranger. It's clear to me that so many people are out there looking for the right person to fit around their logistics. This is true for most of us, from Timothy and Josh from Phantogram to Alex and myself. I feel for him, this gorgeous man, who wants to connect with women but knows he has a time limit imposed by his career in polo. I understand his situation, and I enjoy kissing him between getting to know a bit more about him.

By this time, it's close to 4:00 am, and I have a 6:45 am train back to the city. I tell him, bluntly, that his conversation is good, he's a good kisser, but it's hard for us to understand each other. We fall asleep in each other's' arms and wake to my alarm. As I scramble to rush for my train, it's clear that he wants to stay connected. The frustration of our inability to communicate well continues as he repeats, "Mira, mira." I tell him, "I see you, I hear you, but I just don't understand you."

All at once, I feel as though the totality of the past year's experiences come rushing to me. I don't put restrictions on myself, but I'm quick to realize that what I need in a partner is not in this room. As exquisite and tempting as he is, this is where it needs to end. I'm gathering my things when he nervously asks for my phone number. I tell a little white lie by switching a few of the digits. He calls the number I gave him, and when my phone doesn't start ringing, his face falls.

"Kelly, I don't understand," he says. "I'm standing right here. If you don't want me to have your number, then don't give it to me."

In a rush, I gloss over this awkwardness and my immaturity by telling him that he must have misunderstood my number. But he's pushing a hard line as I pack my bag, asking whether we can hang out in the future, and wanting to know my last name. Distracted, I respond something like, "Well, maybe for the summer," which he misunderstands. I put him in my phone as 'Polo Hampton,' and he puts me down as 'Kelly Summers'. I can't help but laugh at my life's adventures and secretly hope that Marcos and I can remain friends, but I know I can't get sucked into any sort of a relationship.

On my train ride back to Manhattan, I reflect on the past year of adventures. I realize how much I have grown to understand my own needs and desires. I've come to know and love myself through exploration and mistakes. I no longer judge myself for making claims on the things I want in life. I'm no longer afraid to ask for the things I want.

I think about the universal nature of our aspiration to define the life we want. We often wind up envisioning a restrictive box and then look for a partner that fits in that box. I certainly had that mindset earlier in my life, but I've learned that living without fear and living outside the box of what you think you want, will be the path to what *you* truly want.

If I choose to love you, then I love all of you, no matter where you are in the world or what circumstances you have in your life. I no longer love with the fear of loss or a need for a guarantee. I only love.

Through all of these adventures, I retained my dream of finding my twin-soul. That person could be of any age, and from any country. At various times, I thought I'd found that person, only to find that I was mistaken. These mistakes had to be made, though, and as painful as they were, the darkness only brought the light back to me.

With Michael, despite our strong and immediate connection, I had to learn patience and respect. Jumping from the divorce into another long-term relationship would not have given me the space to rediscover myself. I wasn't strong enough to know what I wanted. I had to find Kelly Green again.

With Timothy, I rediscovered my voice while coming to understand myself as a powerful yet vulnerable woman. His support, contrasted with his assertiveness, gave me an opportunity to know what I want and define my own boundaries.

With Alex, I was reminded to be me, and only me. To live freely and be full of life.

With Jake, I not only awakened my sexuality, but also learned to love boldly and purely. He awakened a sensual side of me that is fragile, yet strong. Because of him, I now own my fantasies and am not afraid to live them out.

Even Josh, the musician, reminded me that I am worthy and beautiful. Feeling beautiful has less to do with age or circumstances. It has to do with a woman listening, and the message may come in the most unexpected form. Many times, we are told we are beautiful, but doubts or judgments get in the way of hearing the message. Learning to listen and receive is essential in any relationship.

My train pulls into Penn Station and I stretch, take a deep breath, and feel settled and confident. I know where I stand and what I want, but I still can't let go of deeper feelings of love and desire. I learn to respect that time is not in my control. As life goes on, I'm more patient.

As the summer ends, I return to Austin, and I'm soothed by the familiarities of daily life. My life in Austin and my children continue to be my world. On an afternoon outing with my youngest daughter, we stop by the toy store, where I allow her to choose one toy. She gravitates toward the stuffed animals, grabbing several at one time. She sifts through them. She is holding two in her arms, looking back and forth.

She looks up at me and says, "Mommy, can I please have two?"

I tell her, "No, one is plenty. You must choose just one."

Still, she begs and pleads for two.

"If one of those is not your favorite, then you haven't found the right one," I say. I am patient as she sorts through the whole shelf of animals, smelling, holding, and kissing several. As she nears the end of her selection, she returns to one of the two original bears she was holding.

"I'm sure now, Mommy," she says. "This is the one I want."

As we exit the store, my phone chimes with a message. I read it and feel my heart skip a beat. It is the moment I've been patiently waiting for.

"Kelly, are you there? I want to see you..."

ABOUT THE AUTHOR

KELLY GREEN was born and raised in Texas, completing her college education at Texas Tech University. She is a divorced mother of four young children. Kelly has spent several years as a high-tech sales professional, publishing several articles on the field. This is her first memoir.